THE GUINNESS
BOOK OF CLOCKS

THE GUINNESS BOOK OF CLOCKS

ALAN SMITH

GUINNESS SUPERLATIVES LIMITED
2 Cecil Court, London Road, Enfield, Middlesex

SERIES EDITOR: GEOFFREY WILLS

Editor: Beatrice Frei
Design and layout: Jean Whitcombe
Copyright © Alan Smith and Guinness Superlatives Ltd, 1984

Published in Great Britain by
Guinness Superlatives Ltd, 2 Cecil Court, London Road,
Enfield, Middlesex

Set in Bembo 10/11 pt
Filmset by Fakenham Photosetting Ltd, Norfolk
Printed and bound in Spain by Mateu Cromo Artes
Graficas, S.A. Pinto (Madrid)

British Library Cataloguing in Publication Data
Smith, Alan, *1925 Oct. 31*
    The Guinness book of clocks.
    1.   Clocks and watches—Dictionaries
    I.   Title
    681.1′13′03   TS5407

    ISBN 0–85112–225–6

Acknowledgements

In addition to thanking those individuals, organisations,
museums and galleries mentioned in the captions to the
illustrations, the author would also like to acknowledge the kind
assistance he has received from the following:

The Antiquarian Horological Society; Mr Alan Bartram;
B. T. Batsford Limited; Mr Dana J. Blackwell; Country Life Books;
Mr Ernest L. Edwardes; Mr Eric Gent; Mr Hans Glauser;
Mr Michael Goodger; Mr Stuart Hall; Mr and Mrs Norman Jaques;
Miss Alison Kelly; Mr J. D. Locke; Mr K. D. Roberts;
Mrs Rita Shenton; Mr and Mrs J. M. Smith; Miss Denys Thorpe;
Mr J. E. Thompson; Williamson Art Gallery and Museum,
Birkenhead; Mollie Wilson

Thanks are due in addition to Mrs Vivien Pemberton for typing
the manuscript, and to Mr David Griffiths who took many of the
photographs reproduced.

Contents

Introduction

This book is about the evolution of the style and design of clocks as pieces of furniture, and does not attempt to discuss the mechanical aspects of their movements. The fact that clocks are small engineering devices, often of complex construction and great ingenuity, has endeared them to many whose interest lies in the scientific intricacy of their workings, but for most people—including many clock collectors and enthusiasts—the secrets of their mechanisms remain something of a mystery. Over the centuries clocks have taken their place as part of the interior arrangement of the homes into which they have been placed, and in this sense the history of clocks is very much part of the general history of furniture. Rarely have clocks been studied exclusively in terms of their decorative function and as a part of the continuing development of our domestic environment.

The relationship of clock case design to styles and fashions in architecture and interiors is an important aspect of clocks which lies outside the province of the clockmaker, ie the actual maker of the clock movement. A knowledge of fashionable taste and an understanding of furniture design, proportion, the 'rules' of architectural composition and ornament, and an ability to appeal to the purchasing public or a discerning clientele was, and still is, the responsibility of the case designer, a skill far removed from that of the horological engineer. With comparatively rare exceptions such designers have remained anonymous in contrast to our knowledge of actual clockmakers. Important exceptions may be found in French clocks of the 18th century, when the design of cases was considered to be an art in itself, in many ways superior to that of the clock movement which was a necessary but not dominating feature.

The close ties between clock cases, architectural composition and 'art' styles exist at all periods. Thus the Gothic forms of mediaeval church architecture appear in 15th and early 16th century chamber clock frames; the richness of ornament in engraved and gilded bronze, together with Roman architectural 'orders', is the characteristic of Early Renaissance styles of clocks; the ponderous weight of classical architectural forms and sculpture in Baroque clock cases reflect the work of such master architects as Wren and Mansart. So it was with Rococo fantasies, emanating from France, and Neo-Classicism popularised by Adam and his contemporaries in the 18th century, which affected clock case design and other furniture for wealthy families, though these styles were not so much in evidence in the farmhouse and cottage. With the coming of the 19th century a revival of styles in rich profusion appeared, but used in a way unmistakably of their own time. This period is given considerable emphasis in this book because of the numbers of clocks made, the incredible variety of designs and the present availability of examples at a moderate price. Many clocks of 'art nouveau' and 'art deco' style of the present century are valued today entirely because of the quality of their cases, their mass-produced movements holding little appeal.

Although European clock designers followed the major international movements in art and architecture, individual countries expressed something of their own national temperament in the way in which they adapted the current trends. Thus English 17th and 18th century clocks are far less flamboyant than their French contemporaries, being of quiet, polished natural timber in their casework in contrast to the exotic French gilded bronze mounts, rare veneers, inlays of silver and tortoiseshell and later porcelain, marble and coloured enamels. American clocks, coming under the influence of European styles, show both French and English characteristics as well as some Black Forest features, especially in the period preceding the use of mass-production techniques about the middle of the 19th century. Later American clocks, after about 1850, developed strong and naïve forms derived from European original sources but indubitably American in both their materials and construction. At this time American clock factories also made straight copies of English and French clocks, but used cheaper materials such as cast iron instead of slate, or papier mâché instead of marble. The vogue for 'art nouveau' and 'art deco' designs in the 20th century owed more to French than English taste, while the 'arts and crafts movement' on the one hand, and an innate conservatism on the other, produced, with rare exceptions, a far more staid range of clock cases in England at the same period.

The business arrangements between clockmakers and casemakers is an area about which little is yet known. In all periods it would, generally speaking, be true to say that clock movement makers produced clocks and dials in a range of more or less standardised sizes in order that casemakers would know the critical dimensions in which to make their cases. Although certain specially important or unusual clocks had cases individually made for them it would also be true to say that in the 17th and 18th centuries individual clockmakers would commission their own local cabinetmakers to produce the cases. This would account for the regional styles which developed within the confines of a particular country, such as the East Anglian style in England which is quite different from that of the northern parts, in Lancashire and Yorkshire, and different again from the Scottish styles. By the 19th century factory-produced clock movements and dials were made, especially in France, to such universal standards of shape and size that casemakers could simply mass-produce cases on a vast scale, knowing that movements could be obtained to fit them. For the same reason many English 'makers' took advantage of the availability of standard French and German movements and dials, and a group of English wall clocks is known which were fitted with cheap and reliable American movements. The interchangeability of movements and cases can be a cause of much concern for collectors, for substitution and alteration of clocks and their cases has gone on to a considerable extent, most commonly to 'marry' a good quality clock case to a good quality clock, and thus to enhance the value of the final product.

The days when collectors and horological enthusiasts considered that clocks, however fine, were the individual creations of one specialist clockmaker have come to an end. It is now realised that any clock, of whatever period, was the assembly of the work of many craftsmen, the final product bearing the name of the owner of the workshop where it was assembled or, at a later period, the name of the retailing agent. The mechanical parts of the clock were produced by wheelcutters, spring makers, escapement makers, bell makers and so forth, while dial making, either in engraved brass, painted iron or enamelled copper, was the work of a specialist in this trade. Even clock handmaking was the province of specialised craftsmen, though as in the watch trade it became increasingly common in the 19th century to assemble the various skilled men (and sometimes women) under one clockmaking factory roof. This is the situation today, though with the advent of electronic movements the horological trade is changing and is coming into the sphere of electronic engineering. The decrease in availability of skilled mechanical clock repairers and restorers (as opposed to servicing agencies for modern clocks) is evidence enough of the present position. The appearance on the market of a completely new range of 'reproduction' clocks, made in antique styles, is evidence too of the nostalgia which people feel for old and familiar objects, expressive of stability and permanence in an unstable era.

The following is the text of an anonymous letter pasted inside the case of an old American grandfather or 'tall' clock, discovered by Dr D. H. Schaffer of Pittsburgh, Pennsylvania. It expresses the personal and homely feelings which can be evoked by an old clock which, like other well-used objects of furniture, has come to be a member of the family. It illustrates too that clocks, unlike chairs or tables, have a peculiar life of their own, a warmth and personality of unique human value.

'You dominated our parlor, standing as you did much taller than any of the human occupants of the house. Your dignity was immense and your moods steady—you could quiet me from elation just as you could lift me from melancholy. You were a friend to us all, a regulator on the speed of our lives, and a faithful link between a generation now gone and a generation yet to come. You kept reminding us of our place in the scheme of all things with a special finger that pointed to our days and a little harvest moon that travelled in our private heaven. You were a spokesman for time as you whispered a gentle cadence for the marching seconds and rang your bell to mark the passing of each hours parade. You had the special power to lift past into present, to make that which had lived be alive again. You were the voice of my home—may those who follow me listen too, and through the inward searching you inspire, also learn of peace, of beauty and of love.'

THE GOTHIC AGE
Clocks of the Middle Ages

The word 'Gothic' was originally a term of abuse, describing the work of the Goths, or Barbarians, and was employed especially by those who believed that only the classical art of the Greeks and Romans was worthy of emulation. Today the word Gothic, apart from its association with architecture and the decorative arts generally, is often used to describe domestic clocks of the 15th century. We now see these clocks as part of a remarkable flowering of a style of architecture, sculpture, painting, stained glass, manuscript illumination and metalwork which flourished in Europe from about the middle of the 12th century to the end of the 15th century. This period witnessed an evolution of the Gothic style itself, and there were considerable differences in the style from one country of Europe to another. Recognised primarily by its use of the segmental, or pointed, arch in building the Gothic style enjoyed two major revivals—one in the 18th century when it is usually referred to as 'Gothick' and another in the 19th century when, in England particularly, it had a fundamental effect in both religious and municipal building. One might argue that the style has had an unbroken vogue as far as church building is concerned, and for most people today it is the traditional form for the design of churches, while the Gothic 'black letter' in printing, based on calligraphic originals, still exudes an appropriate ecclesiastical flavour.

An alternative name 'mediaeval' or 'Middle Ages' is often used instead of Gothic to describe that period of European history following the Dark Ages, a period of relative stability based on a feudal structure of king, barons and serfs, the authority of the Church and a monastic system which embraced scholarly research as well as religious observance. Within this world the arts flourished on a scale unprecedented since Roman times, and of a quality of craftsmanship unsurpassed. Unlike later periods of European history the craftsman then was not to be distinguished from the artist, since creators of buildings, glass, manuscripts, furniture, sculpture, paintings and other necessary artefacts were thought of as 'makers' without those confusing and often irrelevant ideas which today separate the designer, the craftsman, the artist and the engineer.

From within this enlightened world, between about 1270 and 1300 AD, the idea evolved for a mechanical clock, powered by weights and incorporating an 'escapement' which would measure, by a controlled release of the power, the passage of time. This concept, which developed to meet the needs of an increasingly ordered society, is unlikely to have been the invention of one man. It is far more likely to have been the result of a slow evolution arising from a previous understanding of the use of toothed wheels and pinions (in the gearing, for example, of wind and water mills) and a long process of development of the water clock or mediaeval clepsydra, of which only references and descriptions remain.

Early references to clocks or 'horloges' would suggest that timekeeping instruments were first used in monasteries, and then primarily as

Drawing of an iron-framed striking clock from a 15th-century manuscript

9

alarms to remind the monks of the times of religious observance. Timekeeping in the Middle Ages presents us with complex problems compared with the relatively straightforward 24-hour cycle of today. Until about the middle of the 14th century 'temporary' or 'unequal' hours were used in which daylight (sunrise to sunset) and darkness (sunset to sunrise) were each divided into twelve equal parts. From this it will be seen that the hours thus became longer or shorter (varying from 49 to 71 minutes, which in turn varied according to latitude) as the seasons changed. Perhaps coinciding with the introduction of the mechanical clock, in which such variations would cause great mechanical difficulties (though these were later overcome by the Japanese who employed a similar system until well into the 19th century) a system of 'canonical' or 'equal' hours was substituted to mark the timing of the monastic offices. Although different monastic orders followed different practices, in general the 'nocturns' marked the night vigils at 9.00 pm, midnight and 3.00 am, and Matins came at dawn. Further offices took place at about 9.00 am (Tierce), noon (Sext) and 3.00 pm (Nones) with Vespers at sunset and Compline at nightfall, about an hour after Vespers. To give audible warning of the times of the offices the earliest mediaeval clocks were provided with alarms (such clocks often being known as alarums) which could be re-set as required. Later clocks incorporated striking systems which were arranged to strike the canonical or equal hours, these being three strokes at Prime, two at Tierce, one at Sext, two at Nones, three at Vespers and four at Compline. Mechanisms designed to strike in this way still exist and the system was easily applicable, later on, to the sounding of 2×12 hours as we know them now.

Monastic clocks of the Middle Ages are few and far between. Some of our knowledge is derived from paintings or veneered (intarsia) panels, but the true Gothic domestic chamber clock of the 15th and early 16th centuries, which so clearly evolved from the monastic prototype, has survived in larger numbers. In the early alarums and Gothic chamber clocks the mechanical work may be seen as clearly as in a Victorian skeleton clock, but these early clocks were mostly made of iron. Wheels and pinions, powered by weights, were assembled for the going and striking trains in an 'end-to-end' manner, and an important manuscript by Brother Peter Almanus, written in Rome after 1475, gives a remarkable idea of the variations of systems of working which were used. In all these clocks, however, the escapement was controlled by a bar foliot or wheel balance in association with verge pallets interacting with the crown escape wheel. The clocks were wall-hanging, and in their Gothic styling were made well into the 16th century. Switzerland, Italy, France and Germany were the source of these clocks and there is no evidence that any of this type were made in England, though certainly turret clocks were made there as early as the 13th century.

The frames of Gothic clocks contain many features which owe their origin to the architectural style which first evolved in stone, a style which is to be found in most of the decorated artefacts of the period. Although the decoration bears no relationship to the structural needs of the frame itself (apart from being of a general form to hold the working parts properly) it is worth digressing to see how the architecturally designed forms came about.

Within the Gothic or mediaeval world a universal architectural style was born, its primary motif being the pointed or segmental arch—an architectural unit which probably had its origins in the Saracenic or Moslem world which was famous for its knowledge of mathematics and geometry. The pointed arch is constructed from two segments of a

Gothic chamber clock of architectural form with cusped o-gee arches on the sides, lancet 'window' arcading, buttressed corner posts and cusped Gothic crossings to the wheelwork; dial and bell missing; mid-15th century. *Bourges Museum*

Opposite page
West front of Amiens Cathedral; 13th century with 14th-century additions

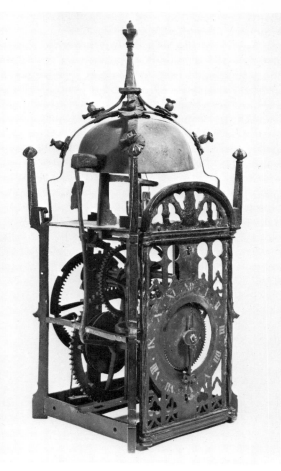

Above left
Gothic iron chamber clock with o-gee supports to the bells, decorative crockets and buttressed corner pillars with finials; 16th century. *British Museum, London*

Above right
Gothic iron chamber clock with o-gee bell supports, decorative crockets and buttressed corner posts with finials; the front is pierced with trefoils and cusped apertures; 15th century. *Clockmakers' Company Museum, London*

circle—a means of spanning spaces architecturally in a fluid way since different widths could be spanned with arches of the same height, or of different heights but of the same width. Such possibilities of building, using relatively small stones, made possible the magnificent vaulted roofing and aspiring vertical structures still to be seen in the great cathedrals of France, Italy, England, Germany and Spain. These buildings rely on an architectural engineering structure of poise and counterpoise, and the arch, as the basis of the structure, is constantly alive, thrusting outwards as the weight it supports presses down. To meet the restless thrusts a system of buttresses, flying buttresses and pinnacles was designed, creating buildings which are essentially frameworks of stone ribs, pillars and arches. Between the spaces in the structure large windows were created in which the glazing was supported by networks of mullions, transoms and tracery in flowing or geometrical forms, following in style the larger architectural concepts of the building itself.

From elaborate and structurally magnificent buildings the elemental forms of Gothic design evolved, based on the pointed arch, rib and panel vaulted roofing, buttresses with widening offsets and pinnacles, variations of the pointed arch including the o-gee, cusped foliations, crockets and finials, all of which permeated downwards to the smaller items of ecclesiastical furnishing such as choir stalls and canopies, chantry screens and canopied tombs, silver altar vessels and embroidered vestments. These were the elements which are found in the framing of Gothic chamber clocks, an architectural style in microcosm but done in wrought iron.

The most notable and characteristic features of 15th and 16th century chamber clock frames are the buttress-shaped pillars which support the corners. As in later Gothic buildings the buttress pillars are angled outwards at 135° to the four sides, generally with three offsets and increasing in thickness to the base. The mouldings on the offsets and on the plinth member also follow architectural precedents. Above the buttresses rise tall, pointed pinnacles which in stone buildings not only punctuated the skyline with aspiring vertical features, but also added considerable weight to the masonry below, to give increased strength and stability. In the clock frames too these Gothic pinnacles surmount the buttress pillars, festooned like their stone counterparts with crockets and finials, but here used merely as a decorative finish.

The pointed arch with its use of arc-shaped segments reached a richness of inventiveness in later Gothic styles of the 14th and 15th centuries, a most notable example being the o-gee arch combining convex and concave curves. In Gothic chamber clocks from the British Museum and the Clockmakers' Company Museum in London this same o-gee feature may be seen in the bell-hanging straps which are mounted above the main frame, and embellished with projecting crockets which have no structural part to play. Here they punctuate and accentuate the design, adding a richness of detail to the profile of the clock as do similar forms on the skyline of a church. Perhaps most clearly related to the contemporary architectural practice are the Gothic chamber clocks from the Victoria and Albert Museum (see p. 33) and a clock from the Bourges Museum in France. Both embrace the most detailed reproduction of architectural features, almost becoming miniature buildings. The clock from Bourges has right-angled buttresses, o-gee arcading on all four sides, 'window' tracery replete with cusped foliations, a spire above with lancet windows and crocketed ridges, terminating in a stiff-leaf foliage finial. Much of the mechanical wheelwork too, though part of the mechanism of the clock, is crossed out, ie cut out to form spokes, in cusped tracery, like the great rose windows which were common in French Gothic cathedrals. The Burgundian clock in the Victoria and Albert Museum, hexagonal in plan, is a veritable reproduction of a monastic chapter house. As well as having plinth and frieze with pierced quatrefoils, and angle buttresses with crocketed pinnacles, it also embraces sculptured figures in niches, mounted on detached shafts on each of the buttresses. Unlike most other clocks of the period (early 16th century) but heralding methods which later became far more usual than iron frames, this very early spring-driven example is in gilded brass. Not all Gothic chamber clocks were of this sumptuous quality, for more simple versions like the one from the Clockmakers' Company Museum of the 15th century, made in Germany, make a Gothic statement in a manner which is far more simple and in many ways more in sympathy with its malleable wrought iron construction. The crockets and finials, in hammered and chiselled form, and the curious off-set pinnacles, present an almost whimsical approach to Gothic design. Its dial plate, however, is pierced with cusped window tracery and articulated trefoils, and the numerals on the dial itself are of Gothic black-letter design.

An important aspect of mediaeval clock frames is their method of construction. The various parts were mostly forged in wrought iron, with some details cast, riveted together where parts did not need to be moved for dismantling the working components, and using pinned mortise and tenons when they did. Some of the frames are entirely riveted except for the bars which support the wheelwork, these bars having pinned or wedged tenons to secure them. No screws whatsoever

Basic frame of a Gothic iron chamber clock showing the principal structural members, with elaborate buttress offsets and finials

Above left
Iron turret clock showing simple buttress offsets and finials of Gothic derivation; from Cassiobury Park but possibly made for the Abbey of St Albans; 14th century. *British Museum*

Above right
Carillon turret clock with elaborate Gothic frame, cusped arcading and parapet, moulded square corner pillars; 1542. *Nederlands Goud-, Zilver-en Klokkenmuseum, Schoonhoven*

were used in these early clocks, and Mr H. G. Hammond [*Antiquarian Horology* (Vol 10 pp. 336–339)] has shown how a clock, consisting of only nine frame elements, fits together by means of an ingenious system of interlocking joints. In its whole construction it has only two taper pins to complete the whole assembly, even these not being seen when the clock is hanging against a wall with its dial plate in place.

Little is known about the workshop conditions under which Gothic chamber clocks were made. By the 15th century many were designed for secular use even though they followed on from a basic style developed in the monasteries. As far as is known no clocks of this type were made in England, though many of the much larger turret or tower clocks were of English manufacture, dating back to the 13th century. On the Continent the guild system of trade control in clockmaking was operating by the 15th century, of which more will be said in the following chapter.

It has often been written that the original clockmakers were blacksmiths, accustomed as they were to working in wrought iron. The art of iron clockmaking, however, required far more than a knowledge of working the metal to shape horseshoes, ploughs or parts for agricultural vehicles, and the skills required are far more akin to those necessary in producing armour, weapons and especially firearms. Mathematical knowledge was required and an understanding of wheelmaking and gearing, and the ability to divide accurately the circumference of wheel blanks to produce efficient teeth and pinion leaves. Moreover, the architectural quality of the finely and delicately made cases of the clocks discussed in this chapter suggests craftsmanship of a high order, combined with an understanding of contemporary design. As soon, therefore, as monastic and later chamber clocks were made, specialised expertise in these fields developed, rapidly becoming organised in craft guilds.

One aspect of mediaeval clockmaking which has not been mentioned is that of turret, or tower clocks. These are the clocks whose generally large movements are housed in towers, where the sound of their striking mechanisms will be heard far and wide, and where a public dial on the outside of the building could be seen by passers-by. Since most turret clock movements are never seen by ordinary citizens, ornamental frames are generally rare, though some in fact had architectural features related to those which have been mentioned for chamber clocks. As the movements of turret clocks in the Middle Ages were generally rectangularly framed using wrought-iron bars, they are known as bird-cage clocks, the corner posts occasionally being shaped with buttress offsets and having decorative wrought-iron pinnacles or scrolled finials. Evidence of this can be seen in the angled corner posts of the famous clock of Salisbury, made in 1382, or in the clock from Cassiobury Park, now in the British Museum. Rare indeed is a turret clock of such elegant architectural detail as the great carillon, or musical clock, formerly in the church of St Jacob in The Hague in Holland, later moved to Utrecht and now in the Nederlands Goud-, Silver-en Klokkenmuseum at Schoonhoven. Built in 1542 its frame is 8 ft 6 in (259 cm) long, 7 ft 9 in (236 cm) high and 5 ft 3 in (160 cm) wide, with four massive square corner columns incorporating architectural offset mouldings, the horizontal top member being decorated above with Gothic cresting surmounted by trefoil finials and with open cusps, while below the member semi-circular foliated arcading also has open cusps. The complete design of the frame of this clock almost creates the feeling of a chantry chapel or rood screen, more familiarly seen in the interior of a church. Such flowering of Gothic design until the middle of the 16th century was typical of the northern European style, for Gothic in the north lasted much longer than in southern Europe.

In view of the link between the mediaeval monastic system, the ecclesiastical evolution of clock design and the Gothic elements of architectural form which conditioned the shapes of the earliest domestic mechanical clocks known, it is perhaps worthy to finish this chapter with a quotation from the early 14th century concerning clocks and the love of the Church for God. In the closing years of his life the poet Dante Allighieri (1265–1321) wrote of his imaginary journey through *Hell, Purgatory* and *Paradise*, known as the *Divine Comedy (Divina Commedia)*. In Canto X of *Paradise*[1] he wrote:

'Then as the horologue, that calleth us, what hour the spouse of God [the Church] riseth to sing her matins to her spouse that he may love her,

wherein one part drawing and thrusting other, [the crown wheel operating the bell hammer pallets] giveth a chiming sound of so sweet note, that the well-ordered spirit with love swelleth;

so did I see the glorious wheel revolve ...'

and later in the same book, in Canto XXIV, Dante described the striking work of a clock, which in the mediaeval manner could be seen in its open frame. His words refer to the first or great wheel which scarcely seems to move, and the last part of the striking train called the fly, which rotates rapidly and has a braking action to control the speed of the movement:

'And even as wheels in harmony of clock-work so turn that the first, to whoso noteth it, seemeth still, and the last to fly ...'

[1] Translation by John Aitken Carlyle.

RENAISSANCE SPLENDOUR
Extravagance and Art

The Renaissance, or 'rebirth' of intellectual ideas, beginning in Italy as early as the 14th century and spreading its tentacles into northern Europe until well into the 17th century, was one of those astonishing developments in life and thought which have profoundly altered the course of human history. Exactly how and why painters, sculptors, architects, writers, philosophers and scientists came to see life and its aspirations in new ways at the close of the Middle Ages is not exactly understood. It was a change in man's attitude to his world which found expression in the arts and sciences and developed an acceptance of the potential of individual minds, realised the value and power of education, enlarged the bounds of learning and free thought, stimulated exploration into the nature of life, of mathematics, anatomy, astronomy, geology, physics and provided the stimulus for exploration, trade and international commerce. It is not surprising that this explosion of ideas also gave rise to the invention of printing from movable typefaces in the middle of the 15th century for it was through the dissemination of ideas in printed form that the Renaissance philosophies spread throughout the whole of the world then known.

In the graphic arts the discovery of the means of expressing space and spatial relationships, the art of perspective, is attributable to a small group of Italian architects and painters, one of whom was Fillippo Brunelleschi (1377–1446) who was also a clockmaker. The idea of being able to express a sense of distance and space on a flat surface (now a normally accepted ingredient of graphic art) epitomised in the 15th century a new approach to life in comparison with the inward-looking, closed world of mediaeval ecclesiastical thought. The philosophy underlying early Renaissance ideas is often referred to as 'humanism'—a devotion to human rather than divine interests, and it was to the ancient world of Greece and Rome, especially the latter, that men of the 15th and 16th centuries in Italy turned for their sources of inspiration.

The Renaissance architectural style began in Italy, surrounded as it was with the ruins of ancient classical Roman buildings, and the first flourishes are seen in Florence where Brunelleschi built new churches such as the Pazzi Chapel (c 1430) for the powerful Pazzi family. The façade of this building, with its semi-circular arch, Corinthian columns, pedimented door, walls divided by pilasters and its overall classical proportions, shows how Brunelleschi had turned his back on the Gothic style and used classical elements inspired by the surviving evidence of Roman architecture. The very first building in the Renaissance style was Brunelleschi's Foundling Hospital in Florence, designed in 1421, but other architects of the period, notably Battista Alberti (1404–72), assisted in the establishment of this new manner of building.

By the end of the 15th century classical ideas in Italian painting and architecture had been thoroughly absorbed, and in 1502 another milestone was reached when Donato Bramante (1444–1514) designed his famous Tempietto, S. Pietro in Montorio in Rome, marking the spot where supposedly St Peter was crucified. Here a small circular pavilion, on a base of spreading steps, surmounted by a dome and cupola, surrounded by a colonnade of Tuscan Doric columns, was to have a profound effect on later building styles throughout Europe, and also, on a miniature scale, the shapes of many gilded bronze Renaissance clock cases. Bramante was later given responsibility for the building of the new basilica of St Peter, which was never completed to his design, but this world-famous church was carried forward by that giant of the Italian Renaissance, Michelangelo Buonarroti (1475–1564), whose particular triumph was its dome. As a painter, sculptor, architect and poet Michelangelo gave physical expression to a style which is known as High Renaissance, the ultimate development of an outlook based on classical ideals.

By the middle of the 16th century, in Michelangelo's later years, a development of High Renaissance took place which is known as Mannerism, affecting architecture, painting and the decorative arts alike. Making full use of Roman prototypes, but in a way which exploited virtuosity of execution and highly decorative surface qualities, the older more restrained classical ideas of Brunelleschi, Bramante and the young Michelangelo gave way to unbridled freedom in which the ancient Roman design elements were re-modelled, in an exotic manner and with individual expression. Typical of the men who worked in this Mannerist idiom was Benvenuto Cellini (1500–71) a sculptor and goldsmith whose *Autobiography* gives a compelling account of life amongst the powerful families and Church of Renais-

St Peter's Church, Rome; view from the choir end showing Michelangelo's dome

sance Italy, and also reveals much of the method of working of a 16th-century goldsmith. Cellini's boastful, swaggering, exuberant and amoral account fully reflects his 'Mannerist' approach to his art, in which classical Roman ideas are worked into exotic, fanciful and highly personal forms. In the same way Mannerist painters such as Michelangelo (in his later life), Tintoretto (1518–94) and El Greco (1541–1614 born in Crete but trained in Venice and lived in Toledo) introduced distortions to the human body, to heighten the drama and expression of their paintings. In the hands of great artists such distortions of classical standards produced works of universal power, but similar distortions of architectural style and ornament often produced, in the minor arts, meaningless symbols and ill-digested shapes.

In comparison with the triumphal world of Italian Renaissance art and architecture, the microcosmic world of Renaissance clocks might seem small indeed, but in exactly the same way as Gothic clocks reflected the architectural styles of the Middle Ages, so the cases of clocks of the late 15th and 16th centuries reflected the aesthetic trends of the period, from overall form to minute details of decoration. They were, in fact, architectural or sculptural essays in miniature, sometimes masterpieces, no longer made in dull iron but resplendant in gilded bronze, rich in decorative arabesques and floral and figurative ornament, to grace the palaces and castles of their princely owners. Not only did the finest of Renaissance clocks contain elements of architectural composition, but they were also constructed to contain, in the best examples, movements of great mathematical ingenuity and cunning complexity.

Clockmaking in Italy in the 15th and 16th centuries is known mainly through documents. The *Almanus Manuscript*, mentioned in the first chapter, describes 30 clocks, some made in Italy, already in existence in the 15th century, and there is the precedent of the great clock of Giovanni di Dondi (1318–89) who described his magnificent mechanism in his *Astrario*, which was finished in Pavia in 1364 and which showed the movements of five of the planets and the Sun and Moon. Modern reproductions based on Dondi's manuscript can be seen in various museums, including the Science Museum in London. Another great Italian maker, Gianello Torriano (*d* 1585) of Cremona, is attributed as the designer of a superb clock for the Holy Roman Emperor Charles V, beneath the canopy of which is a statue of the Emperor himself surrounded by figures of Roman deities, standing on plinths beneath semi-circular arches, with Corinthian columns at each angle of its hexagonal base. On many clocks of the 16th century, 24-hour dials are provided, arranged for telling the time in the Italian manner, evidence of extensive Italian influence in clockmaking and timekeeping.

From the middle of the 14th century the Italian timekeeping system divided the day into 24 hours, but each 'day' ended with sunset, or half an hour later after about 1600. Although the hours were equal in length, and thus much more convenient than the 'temporary' hours of the Gothic era, the difficulty was that the time of sunset varied throughout the year and therefore the clocks had to be adjusted two or three times a month as the time of sunset changed. The reason for this system is said to have been that the clock would always indicate the number of hours of daylight left before curfew and the closing of city gates. Retention of this method of timekeeping long after it had been changed in the rest of Europe is said to have retarded the Italian clockmaking industry.

It was not, however, in Italy that the great school of 16th-century clockmaking was centred but in the south German area of Europe where contact with Italy was long-standing through the unity of the

Holy Roman Empire which embraced Germany, Italy and much of the Mediterranean world at that time. The environment in south Germany, with its knowledge of metal extraction and metal-working skills, combined with native technical inventiveness, was ripe for this development, and an astonishing range of domestic clocks was made there in the 16th and early 17th centuries.

The most important clock-producing town of Europe in the 16th century was Augsburg, which became a centre where the arts and sciences flourished under a well developed guild system. The clockmakers did not have a guild of their own, but (as in England later) were incorporated into the smiths' guild, and were also associated with the locksmiths, since many of the metal-working techniques of clock and lockmaking were similar. Controlled by careful legislation the guild admitted apprentices at least twelve years of age. Their first three years consisted of basic instruction in the craft, followed by a period of three, four or more years as an itinerant journeyman before the craftsman's 'masterpiece' could be submitted, on which he had worked for a period

Modern reconstruction of the astronomical clock of Giovanni di Dondi, the original being finished in 1364. Gothic trefoils and claw feet are the only decorative details, derived respectively from Gothic and Classical precedents.
Science Museum, London

of six months. On satisfactory acceptance of his 'masterpiece' clock, the journeyman was admitted to the status of master in the guild, but the whole system was hedged about with numerous limitations of residential eligibility and family connections.

In making his clocks the journeyman clockmakers required the assistance of various other craftsmen for making the elaborate casework. These were woodturners, cabinetmakers, and silversmiths, goldsmiths, coppersmiths and brassfounders, and even packers for the transport of the finished clocks, who were regarded as a separate trade. One Augsburg clock is recorded in which the assistance of a cabinetmaker, a metalturner, a goldsmith, a dialmaker, an engraver and a script-embosser is known to have been needed, as well as a bookbinder for the leather-bound travelling case.

The manner in which clocks were sold in Augsburg and in other clockmaking centres such as Nuremberg, Prague or Strasbourg, would seem to have been divided into two basic methods, either from stock or by commission. In the 16th century a clock was very much a rare and luxurious item and the status of ownership contributed largely to the motives for its possession, especially a unique one with moving figures (automata) and astronomical or astrological indications as well as the mere indication of the time of day. Clocks could therefore be commissioned for particular clients, or more common types bought from the stock of a clockmaker's establishment; one clock in the Victoria and Albert Museum, dated 1582, is known to have been presented by Mary Queen of Scots to her lady-in-waiting.

The most important technical aspect of south German clocks of the 16th century is that they were powered by coiled steel springs, unlike the weight-driven clocks of the Middle Ages. Exactly when steel springs were first introduced for powering clockwork is still a matter of conjecture, but most authorities now accept that they were first employed about the middle or third quarter of the 15th century, and the association of torque equalising devices with springs (the stackfreed and fusee) was well known by the time that the Augsburg craftsmen were making their clocks. Because of the portability of spring-driven clocks their forms became far more varied than the weight-powered versions, giving their makers freedom of expression of which they took enormous advantage.

In one major group of south German clocks, the basic arrangement is that the movement and dial lie in a horizontal position, to be viewed from the top. Small feet sometimes support the case which might be cylindrical or drum-shaped, square or hexagonal, and they are invariably decorated with engraving, sometimes richly furnished with cast and pierced ornament, and mostly gilded. The dials, either 12, or 24-hour Italian style (or both) normally only have one hand, and at the hours small projecting knobs or 'touch pieces' assisted in finding the time after dark, the touch piece for XII being larger than the rest. These horizontal clocks are sometimes found with alarums, the alarum mechanism being housed in a separate case, supported on brackets clipped to the outer edge of the dial and triggered by means of a lever which is released by the main dial hand. A good example of a drum clock attributed to Paulus Grimm of Nuremberg and dated 1576 is in the British Museum. Edged on frieze and cornice with classical mouldings, its sides are alive with grotesque masks and scrollwork in the late Renaissance Mannerist style, while the eight concentric dials indicate the hours either I to XII or 1 to 24, the Moon's position in the Zodiac, the age and phases of the Moon, the Sun's place in the Zodiac and the prevailing month of the year.

Hexagonal table clock made by Gianello Torriano for the Emperor Charles V; a figure of the Emperor is seen below the canopy while Roman deities surround the base between Corinthian columns; mid-16th century. *Württembergisches Landesmuseum, Stuttgart*

Another clock from the British Museum is a square table clock in a sumptuous gilded case standing on four lion feet (which are probably not original) and known as an Orpheus clock. On the outside of the case a continuous casting in relief represents episodes in the life of Orpheus, a mythical poet who supposedly lived before the time of Homer, who was highly regarded by the Greeks. Presented by Apollo with a lyre he enchanted with his music not only the wild beasts but also the trees and rocks of Olympus. Orpheus, according to the legend, married the nymph Eurydice who, having died from the bite of a serpent, descended into the underworld where Orpheus went to find her. Orpheus so charmed Pluto and Persephone with his music that Eurydice was allowed to follow her husband back to earth on condition that he did not turn his head to look at her. Unable to resist the temptation he did turn round and Eurydice was spirited back to the infernal regions for ever. Both the charming of the beasts and the ill-fated return of Eurydice are worked into the frieze of the clock in low or bas-relief, the bearded Orpheus sitting on the stump of a tree playing a foot lyre, while the bemused animals, birds and trees link the sequence with the figure of Eurydice emerging from the rocks, from which smoke and flames also burst forth. This Orpheus legend formed the subject of many Renaissance sculptured reliefs or frescoes, but the prototype for this particular version has been shown by the late P. G. Coole and E. Neumann [*The Orpheus Clocks* (1972)] to have come from a series of engravings by Virgil Solis, a Nuremberg engraver who died in 1562.

To have interpreted an engraving as a gilded bronze relief, and one which could be repeated for the panels of a number of clocks, an original pattern, probably carved in wood, was first produced. From this wooden master a negative mould was taken which in turn was used to make a positive wax relief. The wax positive, of the thickness of the final casting, was embedded in fireclay. On heating the mass, the wax melted out to be replaced by molten bronze. The final cast surface was finished with punching and chasing before the final gilding was applied. Such finishing of bronzes is mentioned by Benvenuto Cellini in his famous autobiography, written between 1558 and 1562, in his description of the casting of the head of Medusa which was to lie at the feet of his splendid figure of Perseus in Florence:

> 'The first cast I took in my furnace succeeded in the superlative degree, and was so clean that my friends thought I should not need to retouch it. It is true that certain Germans and Frenchmen, who vaunt the possession of marvellous secrets, pretend that they can cast bronzes without retouching them; but this is really nonsense, because the bronze, when it has first been cast, ought to be worked over and beaten with hammers and chisels, according to the manner of the ancients and also to that of the moderns as have known how to work in bronze.'

Another form of spring-driven table clock, frequently described as a tabernacle clock, was made in south Germany in the 16th and first half of the 17th centuries, in which the movement was mounted vertically with its dial on the front in the modern, conventional way. Such a clock is illustrated from the British Museum, and of its kind it is exceedingly plain compared with the elaborately engraved types which were far more usual. The illustration shows the use of architectural motifs, and particularly the basic construction of the clock with its four internal corner columns. Other features which appear on the gilded bronze case of this clock are the classical arcaded drum surrounding the bell, and the balustrading between the corner finials which was essentially a High

Right
Drum clock in gilded bronze attributed to
Paulus Grimm of Nuremberg; the
complex astronomical dials above are
surrounded by ornament in the
Mannerist style; 1576. *British Museum,
London*

Below left
Square gilded bronze table clock fitted
with a detachable alarm mechanism; the
outer sides are adorned with reliefs
depicting scenes from the Orpheus
legend; the scrolled brackets of the
alarm display Mannerist features. South
German, late 16th century. *British
Museum, London*

Below right
Table clock in gilded bronze with the
sides removed to show the movement;
sometimes known as a tabernacle clock.
South German, about 1600. *British
Museum, London*

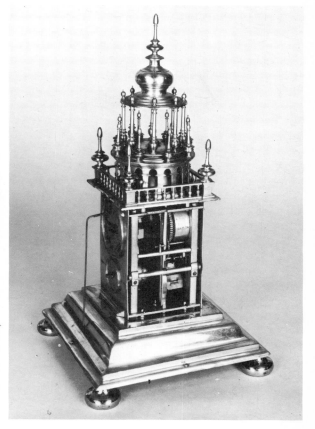

Renaissance feature in Italian architecture. The wealth of metal-turned finials which decorate the tabernacle work suggests an innate pleasure in the skill and variety of metal turning. A feature in this clock which is not to be found in examples from northern Europe is the extra dial below the main one, to mark out the quarter hours. This type of dial may still be seen on church tower dials in Austria and southern Germany.

The practice of adding extra dials and of providing far more information than the time of day, may be seen in a clock now in the Science Museum, London (see p. 33). Although similar in general proportion to the British Museum clock it is far more elaborate, with figures, scrolls, flowers and leaves engraved on the sides and embossed on its broad, 'cyma-reversa' sectioned base, and the details of the tabernacle work above are different too. The corner columns are of the Tuscan 'order' which was one of the most used types in Roman building, with plain unfluted shaft, a cushion-moulded capital and (unlike the Greek Doric from which it was derived) a moulded base member. On the main centre dial is an astrolabe, geared to the clockwork and indicating through its pierced rotating plate or rete, the altitude (the vertical angle) and the azimuth (the horizontal angle relative to the observer's meridian) of the Sun, Moon and certain stars in the heavens at any given time. The positions are indicated by a number of pointers on the rete, read against the tympanum or fixed plate behind it, various plates being made and fitted according to the latitude in which the clock was to be used. Other subsidiary dials give the Dominical Letter for the year (a letter of the alphabet from A to G, calculated by assigning a letter to the first Sunday in January each year, and used for ecclesiastical purposes in establishing the date for Easter), the number of the quarter hour last struck, the number of the last hour struck (either I to XII or 1 to 24), the day of the week, the position of the Sun in the Zodiac and, of course, the time of day on the main dial which also gives the Moon's age and its monthly phases.

The astronomical indicators and other complex readings on clocks of this kind, shortly after 1600, provide clear evidence of the advance of science and mathematics by this time, even though the prime movers of the clockwork were still in a limited state of development, and for accurate timekeeping thoroughly unreliable except when frequently reset by stellar or sundial observations. The astrolabe and its principles were well known in Europe by the early 16th century, and evidence suggests that knowledge of the movements of the heavens and their mechanical indication went back to the Greeks before the days of Christ.

Clocks of the Renaissance were not simply for telling the time of day, but their religious and astronomical indications provided a small, mechanised model of the universe and the harmony of its movements which was believed to have intimate and important associations with the life on earth of individual people. Even today, in our modern world of complex technology, the astrological pronouncements of the daily papers and magazines are avidly followed: how much more important were mechanical means of indicating the calendar, the movements of the stars, the religious cycle of Feast Days, the days of the week and month, in the 15th and 16th centuries, when centralised information sources did not exist. No wonder, therefore, that these mechanical marvels were housed in sumptuous cases of gilded bronze or silver-gilt, and were the prized possessions of noblemen and scholars.

The richness and resourcefulness of 16th-century south German clockmakers is shown also in their figure clocks, often equipped with complex moving parts to actuate the figures, known as automata. Most

Opposite page
Ship or nef clock made for the Emperor Rudolf II in Prague, probably by Hans Schlottheim; part of the dial can just be seen against the poop deck; completed 1581. *British Museum, London*

unusual of all are the great ship clocks or nef clocks such as one in the British Museum. Probably made in Prague, completed in 1581 and attributed to Hans Schlottheim (1547–1625) the dial of this masterpiece is extremely small, insignificantly placed at the rear of the main deck, against the poop. The hours and quarters are struck by models of mariners in two crows' nests on the main mast, and the whole ship could proceed, under its own power, along a dining table and with a rolling motion, while a small organ within played a fanfare, and a procession of mechanical courtiers moved in front of the throne of the Holy Roman Emperor. This intriguing bauble offered little to the progress of serious horological study, but its richness and luxury epitomise perfectly the self-indulgence and vanity of the Renaissance world, and yet in its very ingenuity it marks a point of progress in the evolution of mechanical ideas.

European clockmaking was not confined, in the 16th and 17th centuries, to the south German area in spite of the supremacy it achieved. In France extremely fine clocks were made in such important centres as Blois, Paris, Rouen and elsewhere. They were of the same general style as has been described for German clocks except that square and hexagonal table clocks were normally made with their movements arranged horizontally 'in tiers', the going train above the striking below, but the dials presented in a conventional frontal manner. A small hexagonal clock of this type from the British Museum of domed architectural form (not unlike the western towers of the church of St Michel, Dijon, begun in 1537) with dado, frieze and cornice, has engravings of Mercury, Venus, Mars, Jupiter, and Saturn on the five sides not occupied by the dial. Perhaps the tall hexagonal form of these clocks was indirectly inspired by classical buildings such as the Tower of the Winds (1st century BC) in the Agora in Athens, of octagonal shape and having been used itself for timekeeping instruments and sundials; but the hexagonal or octagonal form is a natural architectural shape, leading to the crowning of a tower with a dome.

Of marked architectural form is another French clock in the British Museum, again hexagonal and dated 1545, but in a case illustrating the Roman derived style of superimposing one architectural 'order' above another. The lower order consists of semi-circular arched openings between three-quarter fluted Corinthian columns, one of the arcades exposing the dial, the others being filled with pierced floral frets. In the upper level the six sides, divided by Corinthian pilasters, are set with Roman half-length figures peering out from roundels, and above the sides triangular pediments complete the design with turned finials between. This clock is no longer complete, for the dial at the top giving lunar information is missing, but it incorporates striking work and alarm, and a dial for the day of the week.

French spring-driven clocks with horizontal drum cases and alarms mounted above, globe clocks, figure clocks, monstrance clocks are all known, heavily ornamented with Renaissance designs originally derived from Roman prototypes but subject to Mannerist deviation, and relying on printed source designs from master engravers such as Virgil Solis and Étienne Delaune who had worked with Benvenuto Cellini. Rarely, however, can original source designs be matched exactly with engraved decoration on clocks, suggesting that the clock case decorators relied more on the spirit than the letter in embellishing their cases. Influence in Europe spread rapidly as master craftsmen moved from court to court. A well-known example is that of Cellini who worked in France for several years (1540–45) for Francis I.

Against this background of 16th-century European Renaissance magnificence must be seen the early art of clockmaking in England which came later and which, by comparison, is 'provincial' in character and restrained in style. Domestic clockmaking in 16th-century England appears to have been very limited, and most clocks belonging to the Royal household were of Continental make, either German, French or from the Netherlands. Like his European counterparts, King Henry VIII was a man most interested in the arts and in timekeeping and astronomy, and employed a Bavarian, Nicholas Kratzer, a friend of the painter Holbein, to make and attend to his clocks. In the *Wardrobe Inventory* of Henry VIII the following description of a clock may refer to one purchased from abroad, or possibly made in London:

'one Cloke of Iron havinge doores of copper and not guilte, with three belles and two men that striketh the howers upon the toppe of the bell. An egle gilte set upon a case of Iron colorid redd with three greate plometts of copper and thre small plomettes to the same. And the same clocke havinge the change of the mone upon yt.'

This clock was clearly a wall-hanging weight-driven item with hour and quarter striking, and might well have been like that seen in Hans Holbein's painting of the English statesman and one-time king's favourite (but later executed) Sir Thomas More. The hanging clock as a type was, however, to flourish in England as we shall later see.

Spring-driven table clocks of English make in the 16th century do exist, but they are very few. A fine example made in the French style in the British Museum is signed by Bartholomew Newsam (d 1593) but in spite of this signature might still have been an importation. Newsam himself was appointed as clockmaker to Queen Elizabeth I in 1572. A particularly interesting example, perhaps with a French imported case, is a small gilded drum-shaped and domed table clock, now in the Clockmakers' Company Museum, London, signed by the Englishman Henry Archer, and made about 1625. A 16th-century maker of Flemish extraction, living and working in England, was Nicholas Vallin (1565?–1603), whose spring-driven clocks which still exist are hardly different from the ubiquitous horizontal drum clocks mentioned earlier. The most important clock known by Nicholas Vallin is his

Detail from a painting by Hans Holbein of Sir Thomas More and his family, showing a wall-hanging, weight-driven clock of the 16th century. *Nostell Priory, Yorkshire*

Drum-shaped table clock in gilded bronze with engravings of hunting scenes; pierced dome below the dial. The case may be of French make but is signed Henry Archer; about 1625. *Clockmakers' Company Museum, London*

weight-driven clock in the British Museum. Probably designed to stand on a hollow plinth or pedestal down which the weights could drop, it is dated 1598 and is the earliest known domestic carillon or musical clock. This steel-framed masterpiece plays tunes on 13 bells before each hourly striking sequence, with shorter pieces of music at the quarters and half hours. Most important, in the context of case design, is the almost pure classical architectural framework of steel and brass, its finely proportioned Tuscan Doric columns of Roman style and parapet pediments being of remarkable refinement and simplicity for its date. It must be remembered that a pure knowledge of classical styles had already entered the field of English 16th-century architecture, originating at first through the work of a north Italian architect called Sebastiano Serlio (1475–1552) and then through a most important design book *The First and Chief Groundes of Architecture* published by John Shute in 1563, the year of his death. Other books, such as the works of the 1st century Roman writer Vitruvius, were also available in England during Henry VIII's reign, creating a transitional move towards classical design which is the hallmark of the Tudor Renaissance, replacing the outmoded Gothic.

Nicholas Vallin's carillon clock brings us to the last clock type in the

present chapter, to the first true English chamber clock or lantern clock, a direct successor to the European tradition. The English wall-hanging lantern clocks appeared about the second quarter of the 17th century, and like the Vallin clock, their main frames were supported by four corner Tuscan Doric columns, normally in brass, connecting two square horizontal plates which in turn supported bars to carry the wheelwork of the movement, the bars being held in place by wedges in a continuation of the Gothic tradition, no screws being used. Also like the preceding Gothic clocks the wheel balance for the escapement was beneath the top-mounted bell and mostly hidden by a parapet of pierced brass frets. The lantern frame type is often known as a 'four poster' or 'bird cage', though the latter term is now usually reserved for iron constructions of this basic design, entirely hidden inside a wooden case. The name lantern is most clearly understood when one sees the frames of these clocks with their dials, side doors and movements removed, but some authorities believe that the name lantern is a corruption of 'latten', the old name for alloys of copper, tin, zinc and lead used in thin sheet form such as clock dials and sides. Certain features in 16th-century German and French clocks survive, such as the four corner baluster-turned finials and the central finial above the bell, held in place with

Above left
Weight-driven musical clock in steel and brass. This clock case is important in its use of Roman Tuscan columns and Classical pediments made in England before the end of the 16th century. Note also the illusion of perspective in the engraved dial plate. By Nicholas Vallin, dated 1598. *British Museum, London*

Above right
Lantern clock in gilded brass, signed by John Peacock and Henry Stevens, dated 1620. This clock is thought to be the earliest dated English lantern clock recorded. *Merseyside County Museum, Liverpool*

metal straps; the single steel hand on the dial; the broad proportions of the Roman dial numerals; the ball or rounded feet which had their origins in spring-driven table clocks; and the overall classical proportions. The detailed dial engraving and the forms of the pierced upper frets, however, had significantly changed, and they owed their stylistic origins to Holland.

During the later part of the 16th century, in Queen Elizabeth's reign, several thousand Protestant refugees had arrived in England from France, bringing with them their native skills. This foreign influence was not new, for as we have seen, it also reached England through the medium of pattern books. But it was the physical presence of many 'Clockmakers straingers from beyond the Seas' that affected the small group of London clockmaking craftsmen, and led to fundamental changes in the decoration of clock cases.

An important milestone in the 17th century, as far as England was concerned, was the founding of the Clockmakers' Company. As early as 1622, documents show that there were only 16 watch and clockmakers in London, and that they were coming under pressure from 'a multiplicitie of Forreniers using theire profession in London'. Some of these intruders (though by no means all), were refugees, and the clockmaking Freemen, by 1627, opposed their intrusion by appeal to the Blacksmiths' Company, to which they then belonged, and at the same time also attempted to separate themselves from the Blacksmiths, believing themselves to be a completely separate trade. Although their pleas to become independent were rejected by the Blacksmiths' Company at that time, they eventually petitioned the Crown, and their Charter was finally granted in 1631. The problem was by no means entirely solved, for many horological craftsmen were already members of other London companies, and wished to remain so. The end of this long struggle for separate and independent recognition of all those involved in 'trading in clocks, watches, alarums, sundials, casemaking, graving and mathematical instrument making' did not come about until 1765.

The importance of the date 1631 for us today, when the struggles of the early London clockmakers to protect their trade are but largely of academic interest, is that it marks a point at which England, like her neighbouring countries of Europe had done many years previously, was to start a native style and quality of clockmaking and one which, for a time, would surpass all others.

The Dutch poet Jacob Cats (1577–1660), ambassador to England in 1657 and ranking high in Dutch literature, recalled an old French proverb which makes a worthy end to this chapter, for in the historical development of clocks, as in life itself, it is necessary to keep starting all over again.

> *Horloge entretenir,*
> *Jeune femme à son gré servir,*
> *Vieille maison à réparer,*
> *C'est toujours à recommencer.*

which may be freely translated as:

> *To keep a clock going,*
> *To please a young girl,*
> *To keep an old house repaired,*
> *One must keep starting again.*

ART AND SCIENCE
Tradition and Revolution

From the south German school of the 16th and early 17th centuries our story of clockmaking now moves northwards, to England, France and Holland, where the greatest advances in horology took place in the 17th and 18th centuries. In England and Holland particularly, the most important single event which was to revolutionise the art and science of mechanical timekeeping was the application of a pendulum to control the motion of a clock, an event which not only altered the outward appearance of clock cases but also stimulated the growth of the clock-making industry. Another important change which took place in the 17th century was the use of timber for the complete construction of clock cases, especially during the second half of that century, in contrast to the use of iron, steel, polished and gilded bronze which were used during the Gothic and early Renaissance periods. The importance of the pendulum and the use of timber in casework will be dealt with later, but we must first look at the continuing Renaissance tradition and its effect on domestic clocks of the 17th and 18th centuries.

One completely metal-framed and cased clock which persisted as a continuation of the old tradition was the brass-cased lantern clock which reached its apogee about the middle or third quarter of the 17th century. Although many were later converted to pendulum control, or made as such, especially in country areas where the type survived until well into the 18th century, the London-made versions are generally of 17th century date. A good example illustrated here is by Thomas Fenn, inscribed 'Neere ye New Exchang' on the dial plate centre, inside the chapter ring. Thomas Fenn is recorded as having been a member of the Clockmakers' Company from 1657 to 1687. The New Exchange, now long since gone but originally in the Strand, London, and built in 1608, indicates that his retailing premises were to the south and west of the traditional clockmaking area in the City of London, and close to the fashionable City of Westminster where prospective wealthy clients were most likely to be found. It is possible that the 'New Exchang' was, in fact, the newly built Royal Exchange at the intersection of Thread-needle Street and Cornhill, rebuilt by 1671 after the Great Fire of 1666; but the style of the clock suggests a date somewhat before that, and of the period about 1650–60.

The upper stage of the Fenn clock consists of the bell which is suspended from a crossing of four brass straps, giving the general appearance of a dome in rather the same way as the dome had become a dominant feature of Renaissance architecture. The bell-supporting straps are attached to the main frame by means of projecting pins which fit into holes drilled on the insides of the four corner finials. The square top plate of the main clock frame is pierced to accommodate various parts of the movement, these being screened from view by three pierced ornamental frets which are screwed to the top plate edges. These frets are decorated with inter-twined dolphins and highly stylised flowers and leaves, probably derived from tulips, the whole design being rather crudely engraved, especially in contrast to the much more sophisticated

Lantern clock with Tuscan corner columns, dolphin frets, turned finials and tulip-engraved dial plate; signed Thomas Fenn (London); about 1660

Drawing of a Roman capital from the Villa Colonna, Rome, showing the decorative use of dolphins in architecture; drawing by John Baxter, about 1760. *National Gallery of Scotland, Edinburgh*

engraving of the main dial centre which is beautifully worked with tulips and leaves, three-dimensionally shaded in a naturalistic manner. This uneven comparison between the frets and the dial immediately suggests that the frets were 'bought in' from a brassfounder, while the dial was executed by a master engraver who specialised in high quality dial work of this type. The conventional arrangement of crossed dolphins in the frets was one of the most popular devices used in English lantern clocks, the origin of which is not precisely known. Since dolphins frequently appear in Greek vase painting and were absorbed into later Roman architectural ornament, it would seem possible that these forms travelled to England by the same route as the general style of Renaissance metal-framed and cased clocks, ie from Italy via France.

To return to the Fenn clock, the delicately swelling corner columns of Roman Tuscan design are screwed to the corner finials and ball feet, incorporating the top and base plates, and the two rear feet are pierced on their backs with holes which formerly held spikes to prevent the clock from swinging sideways when it was hung on the wall; in early versions the spikes were usually riveted to the iron back-plate and not to the main movement frame. Most of the early lantern clocks were suspended from an iron loop or stirrup fixed to the top frame plate, but many later lantern clocks appear instead to have been provided with a wooden wall bracket. Not all the frets on these clocks were of dolphin design, many early examples having what are known as heraldic frets, and some also had frets composed of pierced scrolls, not unlike the parapet ornaments which appear on late Elizabethan buildings, from which similar style source they are undoubtedly derived, originally coming from Holland. The lantern clock case is completed with thin

Above left
Gilded bronze hexagonal table clock of pure architectural form, with buttresses, figures in niches, pinnacles and crockets, and quatrefoil piercing in the frieze; canopy, bell and dial missing; early 16th century. *Victoria and Albert Museum* (on loan to *British Museum*)

Above right
Table or tabernacle clock in gilded bronze with an astrolabe and other subsidiary dials; the corner columns of Roman Tuscan design and the tabernacle of Mannerist scrollwork with turned finials. South German, early 17th century. *Science Museum, London*

Left
Japanese wood-block print showing adjustments being made to a Japanese lantern clock to compensate for the change in the length of the hours; print by Koryūsai, from a series 'Eight elegant parlour scenes'; about 1770. *British Museum, London*

brass side doors to give access to the movement, pin-hinged to the top and bottom frame plates and having small turn-button latches at the front to hold them closed. Originally, most early lantern clocks had a thin sheet iron back-plate, but as many were converted to pendulum action (replacing their brass, verge-controlled wheel balances) these back plates were discarded as they obstructed the mechanism.

In case it should be thought that English lantern clocks were unique to the 17th century, it must be pointed out that at least in the provincial country areas of England they continued to be made well into the 18th century, and that a more or less parallel development took place in Holland where clocks of similar construction, but not identical in decorative detail, were made. The style of Dutch clock referred to is the stoelklok, made originally in Friesland and Groningen and continuing, as a style, until well into the 19th century, some even being made as late as the early 20th century. Like the lantern clock, the stoelklok has its striking and going trains 'end to end' in the mediaeval tradition, and has four corner columns supporting square plates which in turn support vertical bars to carry the wheelwork. The columns of the clock, which in this case are spirally twisted in a tradition dating back to the Italian High Renaissance, are not externally visible as in the English lantern clock, but are only seen through the glazed sides of an outer case. Instead of having an engraved dial plate, the stoelklok dial is painted, but like the lantern the case is ornamented with frets. The arrangement of the Dutch frets is particularly like lantern clock frets, but instead of being pierced and cast brass they are of gilded lead, the one illustrated having a crest and supporters like some English heraldic examples. The stoelklok stands on a small wooden stool with bulbous feet, from which it gets its name, the whole being carried on a wooden wall bracket with a protective 'roof' or hood, sometimes giving it the name of a 'hooded' clock. Although different in many decorative details, there can be no doubt that the lantern clock and the stoelklok belong to the same tradition of four-posted Renaissance structure, but differently finished to suit local regional taste.

The age-old tradition of four-post clock construction survives from the 17th century in France, evolving in its own particular way as a 'country' or provincial style, having the same fundamental lineage as the stoelklok and lantern. The French clocks referred to are the Morbier clocks of the Franche Comté region of France, constructed with four corner columns, usually square in section and unadorned, linking the corners of two flat plates between which the bars for the wheelwork are held. A slight difference of arrangement appears in that the French clock wheel trains for going and striking are side-by-side instead of end-to-end, but the oldest 17th-century examples have corner finials, a bell mounted above, small bun feet and a frontal pierced brass fret. Belonging to the same tradition they show, in comparison with the English lantern and Dutch stoelklok, the different directions in which a primary idea, derived from 16th-century south German origins, could lead. Later the Morbier, more commonly known as the Comtoise, evolved in different ways, and the cast brass frets of the early versions changed to ornamental head-pieces in thin pressed brass, and they were also fitted with fired enamelled dials. Like the Dutch and English clocks mentioned, the Comtoise was a provincial development with the idiosyncratic system of striking the hour twice, once at the hour and again two minutes later. The Comtoise was made in a variety of forms until the beginning of the First World War.

The provincial four-posted lantern frame was made in Spain, in the region of Catalonia, similar in many ways to the Comtoise in France

Dutch stoelklok with twisted columns on the movement frame, painted dial and cast lead frets; no maker named, early 18th century

Opposite page
Year-going, spring-powered mantel clock made for King William III and known as the 'Mostyn' clock; case of veneered ebony with silver and silver-gilt mounts; made by Thomas Tompion, London, 1695–1700. *Photo courtesy of Christie, Manson and Woods Ltd (now in the British Museum, London)*

Above left
French wall-hanging clock with alarm
(pendulum not shown) known as a
Comtoise; the head piece is of thin
pressed brass and the dial of enamelled
copper; signed Louis Badoz, au Puy,
about 1870

Above right
Spanish wall-hanging clock (pendulum
not shown) of similar construction to the
Comtoise; signed Joseph Saldari,
Mataro, late 18th century

and belonging to the continuing tradition of a rural and popular style as
opposed to the far more sophisticated products of courtly and aristocratic circles. A curious, and perhaps unexpected offshoot from this Iberian
development is the Japanese lantern clock, established in the Far East in
the 17th century.

Japan first made contact with the West in 1542, when Portuguese
merchants landed on Tanegashima at the southern tip of Kyushu. Some
years later European Christian missionaries arrived, and for nearly a
century European goods, especially arms and clocks, were carried to
Japan as gifts or for trading. So fascinated were the Japanese in these
strange novelties that they themselves set up their own clockmaking
centres in Tokyo, Nagoya, Kyoto, Osaka and Nagasaki, and copied the
designs brought in from Spain, Holland and Portugal. Of these types
the four-posted lantern frame was an early model, weight-driven and
controlled by a verge and foliot escapement. Although a sudden end to
European involvement came about between 1624 and 1638, when the
last Portuguese were expelled, Japanese craftsmen continued to make
the lantern form of clock in their closed world until the middle of the
19th century, when Japan was again open to the civilisation of the West
through trading contact with Great Britain and America. Another type
of Japanese clock which has certain stylistic relationships with the
lantern is the pillar clock, for here, in spite of the fact that its primary
construction carries the wheelwork between flat plates, in front of the
movement there are two decoratively turned pillars—a relic of the four
pillar style—but in the pillar clock the Japanese made a use of the slowly
descending weight in a way which was very rarely done in the West. A
pointer fitted to the weight indicated the time on a vertical scale which
could be adjusted regularly to accommodate the unusual Japanese
timekeeping system.

A note on the Japanese method of timekeeping will remind us of the
vagaries of the mediaeval European period, when a system of 'tempor-

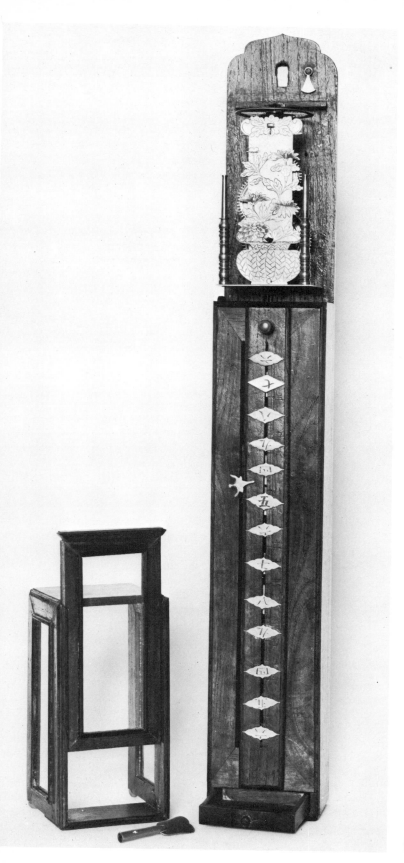

Left
Japanese pillar clock with hood removed
to show the ornamental turned columns;
key with special drawer below; 19th
century. *University Museum,
Manchester*

Below
Japanese hanging clock, referred to as
'Kakedokei', similar in construction to the
European lantern clock; about 1670.
*Courtesy of The Time Museum,
Rockford, Illinois*

Black Forest wall-hanging clock
(pendulum not shown); wooden framed
movement with wooden painted dial;
about 1850

ary' hours divided the complete daily cycle into two basic parts, daylight and darkness, which in turn were divided into twelve equal parts which varied in length as the seasons changed (see p. 33). Similarly, the Japanese divided their periods of daylight and darkness, but into six equal parts which, of course, also changed in length throughout the year. Japanese mechanical contrivances took this problem into account, either by altering the vibrations of the escapement or altering the position, and thus the lengths, of the hours on the dial. The constants, from which all the other timekeeping calculations were made, were mid-day and midnight, numbered invariably as 9. The complete Japanese sequence of hours was numbered 9 8 7 6 5 4 9 8 7 6 5 4 9 etc. The figure 9 was regarded as a mystical number and to obtain the notation given, the six daily and six nightly 'hours' (as we would number them 1 2 3 4 5 6) were multiplied by 9 eg $1 \times 9 = 9$; $2 \times 9 = 18$; $3 \times 9 = 27$ etc., the second figure of this table being the number actually used. In later Japanese lantern and other clocks, complex calendar information was also provided, as was done in western clocks, though the Japanese calendar was far more complex than ours. Japanese lantern clocks with their weights were frequently, though not invariably, mounted on a stand or pedestal, this being particularly important in houses with flimsily constructed walls and screens. The subject of Japanese lantern clocks has been raised here to show how the Oriental lantern clock, the Dutch stoelklok, the French Comtoise clock, the English and Spanish lantern clocks and even the wooden-framed, four-posted German Black Forest clocks of the late 18th and 19th centuries belong to a tradition of construction which can be traced back to early Renaissance beginnings, all variants of the 'bird cage' form, and they all survived for about the same period of time. But now we must return to the mid-17th century to witness vital and basic changes to clocks and clockcase design.

By far the most important invention in the science of mechanical horology was the application of the laws of the natural vibration of a pendulum to serve as a timekeeping standard in clockwork. First conceived as a possible idea by Leonardo da Vinci (1452–1519) and with the laws relating to the natural oscillation of a pendulum subsequently described by Galileo Galilei (1564–1642) in 1602, a clock governed by a pendulum was actually made by Galileo's son Vincenzo in 1649. It was, however, eight more years before the clockmaking fraternity was to see this device used for commercial clock production, and the genius primarily responsible for this was Christiaan Huygens (1629–95), an eminent mathematician, physicist and astronomer who commissioned a Hague clockmaker, Salomon Coster (d 1659) to make pendulum clocks to his design in 1657. A year later a second generation Englishman of Flemish descent, Ahasuerus Fromanteel (1607–92) was found advertising pendulum clocks in London as a result of studies by his eldest son John with Coster during the preceding year. The precise historical details of the far-reaching events of 1657 and 1658 have been described many times, but it is logical to suppose that those universal factors which produced so many scientific, philosophical and artistic giants at this period would have inevitably produced some far-seeing scientist to have applied the principle of the pendulum to clockwork, had it not been Huygens. The important fact is that the clock as a mechanism changed from being a useful though somewhat approximate measurer of the passage of time to being a highly accurate scientific instrument. Although the four-posted, traditional provincial clock survived in many variations and in many countries even into the 20th century, the scientific advances which came with the application of the

pendulum produced a new breed of sophisticated mechanisms, requiring to be housed in cases of equal status, reflecting the most up-to-date trends in architectural composition. The arrival of high-quality pendulum clocks in the 17th century, if not exactly revolutionary, was a turning point in history as important as the invention of printing two centuries earlier, or the harnessing of steam and atmospheric power by that other great 17th-century engineer, Thomas Newcomen (1663–1729) half a century later.

Of the earliest pendulum clocks known, one by Salomon Coster—a Hague clock—in the Rijksmuseum in Amsterdam has a plain, rectangular ebonised case hanging from the wall on two rear-mounted rings. Once established, such Hague clocks, or Haagsklokken, quickly attracted rich ornamentation and architectural design befitting the homes of those sufficiently affluent to afford them, and there is much evidence to show that French styles of decorative treatment penetrated the Netherlands through the incursion of Protestant Huguenot refugees, especially after the revocation of the Edict of Nantes in 1685, which had formerly given the protection of religious freedom when it was originally signed by Henry IV in 1598. High Renaissance French mannerist architectural features, such as the segmental pediment or the broken pediment, appeared above the black wooden cabinets, with flanking pilasters, skeletonised or solid chapter rings on velvet grounds, and the relatively common feature of a bas-relief figure of Father Time with his sickle, scythe and sometimes an hour glass. A glimpse of the architectural composition of the central bay of the Hall of the Marchands-Drapiers in Paris (1655–60) with its broken segmental pediment and flanking pilasters, gives a good indication of the type of contemporary architectural

Above left
Hague clock (Haagsklokje) in wooden cabinet with broken pediment, flanking pilasters and skeleton dial; fitted with an alarm; signed Johannes van Ceulen, Haghe; late 17th century

Above right
Façade of Hall of the Marchands-Drapiers, Paris, now reconstructed in the Carnavalet Museum; the architectural features are similar to those on the Hague clock; designed by Jacques Bruant, 1655–60

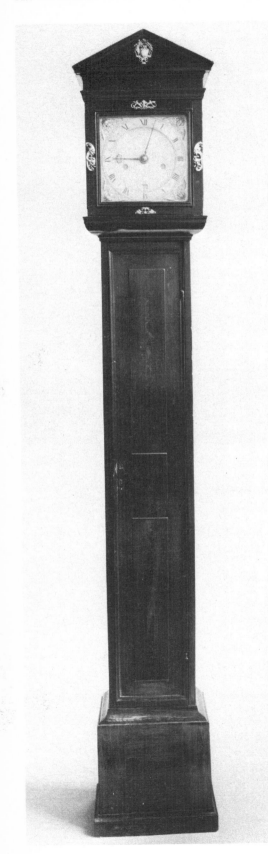

design which such clock cases emulated. The origin of the segmental arch in the European tradition may be seen in Michelangelo's top storey of the Palazzo Farnese in Rome (1548), over a hundred years earlier, in which the segmental pediments crown the lintels of the windows.

The English fashions in architecture and furnishings were never as elaborate as those of her Continental neighbours. Perhaps this was due to, or at least is reflected by, the early endeavours of a famous English architect Inigo Jones (1573–1652). Early in the 17th century he introduced into England a style of architecture that was completely classical, derived partly through his visits to Italy before 1603 and partly on his close study of the buildings and publications of a famous late 16th-century Italian architect, Andrea Palladio (1508–80). Palladio was called upon to design town and country houses in the Roman architectural tradition, such as the Villa Capra at Vicenza, built in 1550–54. A precise and detailed knowledge of the Roman classical orders was obtained by Inigo Jones from his comparison of the drawings in Palladio's *Quattro libri dell'architectura* with the original Roman buildings from which Palladio's measurements were taken. England profited immeasurably by Jones's new design for the Queen's House at Greenwich, built between 1615 and 1622, and the slightly later Banqueting House in Whitehall of 1619–22. In these classical buildings of superb aesthetic purity, Jones established a style known as Palladianism. This was to flourish in the 18th rather than the 17th century, for he was an innovator and prophet. It is perhaps not too far-fetched to suggest that his influence might be traced in those fine early London pendulum clocks of English design, before Baroque exuberance clouded the view.

By the end of the 1650s in England, when the pendulum as a regulating device first came to be used in clocks, a new approach was taken to housing the movement, involving the cabinetmaker working in wood. The first pendulum clocks employed a short pendulum which only required a narrow space in which to swing, but a case was a necessity for protecting the movement from dust and a long trunk for enclosing the weights. These early clocks, therefore, had long and narrow cases which are sometimes known as 'architectural' in style and which continued to be in vogue from about 1660 to 1675 when more elaborate casework was the fashionable standard. Why were these early long-cased clocks of so simple and elegant a form, such as those shown here by Ahasuerus Fromanteel and Thomas Tompion? The answer might be that a clock case in wood, as far as English cabinetmakers were concerned, was an entirely new concept, never attempted before in the history of English furniture. New problems require new and cautious solutions and the simple and yet extremely elegant forms produced, of strictly functional concept, certainly owe something of their design to the newly introduced Palladian manner, yet at the same time they remained quiet and unassuming in domestic interiors to which they were entirely new-comers. The cabinetmaking fraternity had not yet assimilated the longcase form into their general furnishing range, but in their very reticence they produced objects of dignity and style.

This early 'architectural' style of timber clock case was generally in oak, veneered with ebony imported from either India or Ceylon, regarded as a most precious type of timber which polished to a rich deep black, or a close-grained wood such as pearwood which was easily worked and would take a black stain. The tall cases were provided with a long narrow door to observe the weights during winding, while the hood or top member which protected the movement, was made to slide upwards to give access to the dial for winding and adjustment, unlike later longcase clocks which have a pivoted glazed door. The clock by

Opposite page
(*left*) Longcase clock by Ahasuerus Fromanteel, London, in a tall, slender case of 'architectural' design; about 1670. *British Museum, London*
(*above right*) Dial and hood of a longcase clock by Thomas Tompion, London; early winged cherub spandrels and tulip-engraved dial plate; Corinthian three-quarter columns; about 1675
(*below right*) Dial of a longcase clock by Edward East, London; plain matted dial plate and flower-engraved corners; about 1665

Fromanteel and the one by Tompion have their hoods surmounted by a simple triangular classical pediment, with strictly architectural mouldings of frieze and cornice. The only additional ornaments applied were gilded mounts on the Fromanteel, and three-quarter columns with finely worked and gilded Corinthian capitals and bases on the Tompion. A point to notice in these early clocks is the ovolo or wide convex moulding beneath the hood, where it narrows to the trunk, which is one of the hallmarks of 17th century English longcase design.

In their arrangement of the dials, the clock designers of the third quarter of the 17th century were on more familiar ground, for they were working in metal, with a long traditional past, though even here the very earliest examples are plain and simple, but of most elegant proportion. An example signed by Edward East (characteristically in Latin) of about 1665, has its dial plate engraved at the corners and its centre plainly 'matted', while the clock by Tompion, about ten years later, has cast and gilded mounts, known as spandrels, in the form of winged cherubs' heads, and a dial centre engraved with leaves and tulips and similar to many contemporary lantern clock dials. With increased accuracy of timekeeping, these new pendulum controlled clocks were provided with hour and minute hands. By the time Tompion's clock was made, incorporating the anchor escapement with a long seconds or Royal pendulum, dials were provided with a separate auxiliary dial on which seconds were recorded. Engraved and silvered chapter rings, pinned to the dial plates, were narrow and elegant and the blued steel hands of restrained design, enlivened only at the tip of the hour hand, complete the dials of this period of clockmaking which established standards for the next two centuries—high standards which, alas, were not always maintained as the years went by. It is curious how, in many areas of human endeavour, the first solutions were the simplest and the best, only to become degraded by the passage of time.

The last clock to be mentioned in the present chapter is a small, ebony

Below left
Table clock by Samuel Knibb, London, in an ebony veneered 'architectural' case; dial plate engraved with flowers; about 1665. *Clockmakers' Company Museum, London*

Below right
Back plate of the table clock by Samuel Knibb, notable for the elegance of its engraved count plate, pendulum cock, hammer bracket and especially the lettering of the signature. *Clockmakers' Company Museum, London*

veneered table clock by Samuel Knibb of about 1665. Although the weight-driven longcase had the advantage of precision, since the power of a falling weight is invariable at whatever stage of its winding, a spring-driven portable clock was in many ways more convenient. The 'architectural' style of this clock is exactly like the longcase examples we have seen, restrained and refined in its classical manner. Like the Edward East, its dial plate corners are engraved and its dial centre engraved too, like the Thomas Tompion, with tulips, daffodils and lilies. Unlike the longcase, however, which was made to be fixed against a wall, its movement back plate can be seen, and the back plate of the Knibb clock is attached to the front, or pillar plate, with elegantly curved latches which secure the plate to the pillars. The finely scrolled lettering of the signature, the decorated pendulum cock, the striking work count plate and bracket for the striking hammer arbors all add up to a creation of exquisite decorative detail contrasting with a plain area of polished brass of most attractive and restrained appeal.

The early phase of English pendulum clocks has never been surpassed, yet we do not know the name of more than one single casemaker. From the chance discovery of a half-penny token of Joseph Clifton, Bull Head Yard, Cheapside, dated 1663 and found in a crevice in the base of a longcase clock by Ahasuerus Fromanteel, it is assumed that Clifton is the name of one of the casemakers, though there were probably several more, dominated in their designing perhaps by Fromanteel himself. The same lack of detailed knowledge of the clock casemaking trade will dog us further, a commercial reticence which is difficult to understand in view of the superlative nature of many of the cases.

In the first book on clocks and watches published in England in 1675 and entitled *Horological Dialogues in three parts, shewing the Nature, Use and Managing of Clocks and Watches*, the Clockmaker John Smith (free of the Clockmakers' Company in 1674 and died before 1730) wrote on the question of choosing a good clock:

'Observe whether every particular part of it be true and square whether it be clean, smooth and well polished, whether the needle or hand be true filed, and of a neat order whether the hammer strike one [sic] the Bell so true as may cause it to give its sound clear and ful without intermixture of harshness and Jurgelling, and whether the work be generally in all its actions lively, brisk and pleasant, if you find all these in a Clock you may conclude it was made by the hand of a good work-man, and consequently that it is good work, which is alwaies best cheap though it cost dear.'

and as for installing a clock in one's house he goes on to say:

'In setting up long-swing Pendulums, after you have taken them from the coffin [packing case], open it, and make free all things that are fastened ... then in the room it is designed to stand in, seek for some post if possible near the place you desire it should stand at, to which proffer the Clock and case together as it is, which done fasten the back part of the Case with a nail or screw to the post, then hang on the weight according to the marks by the workman given, and set the Pendulum on vibrating, and according to the beating of it you will understand which way to elevate or depress the same to make it beat equal and swing clear of the case: then when you have found it to stand in its true position, fasten it with another nail or two, that it may stand firm and not shake: the same rule that is given for this serves for all other trunck-cases whatsoever.'

BAROQUE EXUBERANCE
Monumental Clockmaking

The Church of the Invalides, Paris; designed by Jules Hardouin-Mansart, 1680–91

The term 'Baroque', by dictionary definition, means 'whimsical', 'grotesque' or 'odd', but it is also the name used to describe a period of European art and architecture which might loosely be bounded by the years 1650 and 1730. In England its beginnings more or less coincided with the restoration of the monarchy in 1660, and in France with the accession of Louis XIV in 1643. The name Baroque is said to have come from the Spanish word *barrucco*, meaning an irregularly shaped pearl, and in its various manifestations throughout Europe it assumed many forms, sometimes of the most extravagant and florid types, especially in its later phases, and often a quality of strong monumentality. In architectural terms the origin of the style was to be found in Mannerism, and the first major works were Italian. Giovanni Lorenzo Bernini (1598–1680) was the first great architectural exponent of Baroque, famous for his colonnades flanking the piazza in front of St Peter's in Rome, embracing space in a manner not previously conceived. In France the architect Jules Hardouin-Mansart (1646–1708) created buildings such as St Louis des Invalides in Paris, which express new spatial groupings of classical elements in a theatrical manner somewhat pompous and individual, while in England probably the greatest monument to the Baroque style is St Paul's Cathedral in London. This familiar yet stupendous building, which although composed in detail of the elements of the classical orders, is arranged in a manner which is pure Baroque, especially as to the design of its general plan in a Latin cross and the form of its dome and twin western towers, with all the whimsicality and distorted grouping of the ancient Roman forms which the style Baroque implies. At the same time it has immense dignity and monumental presence, and it is unfortunate that the original plans for the new streets and spaces which were to be built after the Great Fire of 1666 were not completed, for St Paul's was designed to terminate a vista, to have external spatial presentation with which it unfortunately has never been graced, yet which it needs to fulfil the grandeur of its Baroque concept. Its creator, Sir Christopher Wren (1632–1723) was one of the intellectual giants of the period, and although best known for his work as an architect, he was one of the foremost scientific minds of the 17th and early 18th centuries. Whether, as a young man and newly appointed Professor of Astronomy at Gresham College in London, Wren had anything to do with the designing of the superb classical clock cases by Fromanteel and others we may never know, but that he was interested in horology as in the other sciences there can be no doubt.

To understand the relationships which exist between the most superlative of clock cases and the building styles of the Baroque period, let us start by introducing a magnificent Tompion clock, a year-going, spring driven, striking mantel clock known as the 'Mostyn' clock from its previous ownership by Lord Mostyn, now in the British Museum (see p. 34). Thomas Tompion (1639–1713) was perhaps the most famous and is certainly now the best known name amongst 17th-century clockmakers, and he produced this clock for King William III, who was

St Paul's Cathedral, London; designed by
Sir Christopher Wren, 1675–1710

born in the Hague, the son of Mary, daughter of Charles I, and took the
English throne by invitation in 1689 to replace the deposed Roman
Catholic sympathiser James II. In its elegant and sumptuous, court-
quality casework the clock expresses the characteristics we see in
contemporary buildings, the same mixture of classical orders and
mouldings, the same application of sculptured figures, reliefs and other
extraneous ornament.

Of the many architects and designers who were responsible for
spreading the Baroque style the name of Daniel Marot (*c* 1661–1730) is
at once the most important in terms of interior design and furniture.
Born in Paris, he was the son of the French architect Jean Marot (who
competed for the design of the Louvre in Paris with Bernini and others
in a competition which was adjudicated by Wren on his only major visit
abroad). Daniel left France for Holland in 1685 for religious reasons,
entered the service of the Prince of Orange, and later became Minister of
Works to King William III in England, styled *architecte de Guillaume III,
roy de la Grande Bretagne*. Marot's designs were published as a vast
number of engravings for furniture, interiors, schemes of designs for
sculptors, metalworkers, plasterers and the like, and though there are
but few pieces of furniture which can be attributed to Marot with
certainty, his influence through his published work was immense. In
the present context his style of designing, conceived in the French court
manner of Louis XIV, matured in Holland and spread about in England,
emphasises the international nature of the Baroque style against which

the Tompion clock should be seen. Although the design of the Mostyn clock has tentatively been connected with the name of Marot, it is more than likely that the design was simply influenced by his style, rather than it was actually the product of his hand.

The Tompion Mostyn clock, argued to be the finest spring-driven clock ever made, is a mantel clock of modest size (2 ft 4 in, 71 cm high) but of the most monumental conception of architectural scale, matching the incomparable performance of its mechanical interior. Surmounted by a silver figure of Britannia on the inverted-bell top, flanked by corner finials of a lion, unicorn, rose and thistle and with a central cartouche bearing the crowned royal arms, the upper part of the black ebony case has gilded Roman Tuscan columns with silver capitals on either side, and silver festoons hanging from lion-mask heads. The whole upper case contains the movement and dial and is built on a wider plinth which holds the enormous and powerful springs. The plinth also has bas-relief mounts and a pierced silver fret with flanking cherubs on corbelled seats, amidst flowing ribbons and a wreath of leaves, through which the action of the pendulum may be seen. The whole case stands on four magnificent double scrolled feet, connected to centrally gilded

Designs for tables by Daniel Marot, from a set of etchings called *Nouveau Livre d'Orfevrie*; about 1700. *Victoria and Albert Museum, London*

masks with that most typical of Baroque features, the floral swag. Its superlative quality of gilded metalwork and silver, richly contrasting with the geometric discipline of the straight-lined edges of the black ebony case, cannot be overstated. Here, in the care of a great British institution, to be seen by all, is a clock of the highest possible quality and an architectural masterpiece in miniature.

A glimpse at one or two architectural schemes contemporary with the Mostyn clock will show the same stylistic features which are the core of the Baroque manner. The interior of Christopher Wren's Banqueting Hall at Greenwich was painted by Sir James Thornhill (1675–1734) in an architectural scheme of Corinthian pilasters and capitals, with the Royal Arms and trophies-of-arms in bas-relief, in majestic effect although painted flat, with a trompe-l'oeil sense of illusion. These architectural elements of Baroque theatricality frame Thornhill's paintings like the Mostyn clock case frames its important feature the dial. At Greenwich, in the grand manner, Thornhill represented William and Mary attended by mythological figures of Apollo, the sun god, in his chariot, with Pallas representing wisdom and Hercules emblematic of strength. Here the gods of Olympus intermingle

Part of the wrought-iron screen facing the River Thames at Hampton Court Palace; designed by Jean Tijou, 1695–1700

with the King and Queen of England in a theatrical pageant of splendour and conceit. Magnificence of Baroque design may be seen in other media, in the wrought-iron gates at Hampton Court by Jean Tijou, a French Huguenot immigrant, and in the sculptures of Grinling Gibbons (1648–1720), who was born in Rotterdam but of English parents, whose carvings in wood on the choir stalls at St Paul's provide us with examples of the applied decorative devices of the period, like those on the Tompion clock. The most important point about architectural schemes in this superlative era of Baroque design is that metalworkers, sculptors, painters, cabinetmakers, plasterers and other craftsmen came under the central and unifying control of the master architect/designer. Such must clearly have been the case in designing the cabinet for the Tompion clock. We do not know who designed this case, but who is to say that it was not Wren himself?

The international link between designers and craftsmen of the Baroque period reminds us of French styles, some of which appeared in British design but some being unique to France. One of these was the scroll-footed mantel clock in which lavish use of bas-relief gilded bronze plaques and other decorative details were applied to a round topped case, the door of which was glazed to reveal both the dial itself and the pendulum swinging below. This arrangement had no counterpart in England, for in English mantel and bracket clocks the pendulum was seen from behind and its ornamental extravagance was included on the engraved back plate. Dials in France too were quite unlike their English equivalents for they were designed with white enamel plaques, one each for each separate hour and sometimes a further set of twelve to mark out the minutes. These plaques were fired with an opaque white enamel, like the dials of watches at a later date, on which the numerals were painted in black, with dark blue for the minutes, and fired again to fuse the colours. The separate plaques were attached to a cast brass dial plate designed with spaces to accommodate them, leaving the centre dial of metal with cast and chased designs. The relief decorations, or metal mounts as they are called, on Louis XIV clocks were magnificently produced and included figures of Father Time (Chronos) (no doubt inspired by the Dutch), mythological gods and goddesses, masks, acanthus leaves, frets, finials, lock plates, brackets and pendants. These mounts were sometimes cast and sometimes hammered to produce repoussé effects, but although of many elaborate and varied kinds they were rarely finished with the graver or the file to a quality to be seen in French clocks of the 18th century.

Another form of French clock appearing in the 1680s was the 'dolls' head' design or tête-de-poupée, its complete shape being of oval form like a head, mounted on a moulded base with indented scrolls at the sides. Unlike the arch-topped Louis XIV bracket clocks, dials of the tête-de-poupée clocks often continued the earlier form, having a silvered chapter ring mounted to an engraved dial back-plate, and it was with these clocks that the name of André-Charles Boulle is first associated.

André-Charles Boulle (1642–1732) was one of the most famous of French ébénistes or cabinetmakers, and his name has been associated particularly with a form of decoration known as marquetry, which consequently bears his name. Marquetry consists of decorating the surface of an inferior wood with elaborate patterns of thin wooden veneers, thin sheets of copper or brass, tortoiseshell and sometimes other materials. The method was to 'sandwich' together two thin sheets of different materials which were then sawn through with a very fine fret saw into the desired pattern. After sawing, the sheets were separated yielding the positive and negative parts of a complete flat pattern which

could be assembled together in jig-saw style as two designs, one being the reverse of the other. These two patterns were known as première partie and seconde partie or contre partie, the first being used when the outer or main edge of the design was in tortoiseshell, and the second when it was copper or brass. The most acceptable version, used in the best parts of casework and in the best clocks, was always the première partie, in which the predominant groundwork was tortoiseshell. Boulle marquetry was to be revived again later, particularly in the early 19th century, in England as well as in France. Boulle marquetry was an elaborate and attractive formal ornament applied to the often curved surfaces of tête-de-poupées and Louis XIV bracket clocks and the brackets which supported them. The Baroque manner of marquetry work can be seen to perfection in a pedestal clock signed by J. F. Dominicé in the J. Paul Getty Museum in California, in which the style of marquetry on the pedestal is remarkably similar to the design of Jean Tijou's Hampton Court wrought-iron screen—an imaginative arrangement of leaf forms and scrolls interwoven with straight-line verticals and horizontals—but derived too from ornamental friezes done in classical Roman times.

The longcase clock which had appeared in England in the mid-17th century did not take on in France, though once the superiority of the long seconds pendulum and the anchor escapement (introduced in England about 1670) over the ubiquitous verge and short pendulum was established, it is difficult to understand why this should have been so. French styles very much favoured the pedestal clock which was, in fact, simply a bracket clock mounted on a tall stand whose decoration

Above left
French terra-cotta model of a mantel clock; this is probably a model made for a client's inspection and never had a movement; unsigned, about 1700.
J. Paul Getty Museum, Malibu, California

Above right
French 'tête de poupée' clock from a design by A–C Boulle; Boulle-type marquetry and gilded bronze mounts of a cupid and Father Time (Love conquering Time); made by the Martinot family, Paris; early 18th century. *Wallace Collection, London*

49

French pedestal clock with musical movement; the sumptuous case is veneered with Boulle-type marquetry in tortoiseshell and engraved brass and is elaborately mounted with gilded bronzes; movement by J. F. Dominicé; about 1720–25. *J. Paul Getty Museum, Malibu, California*

Right
Original drawing by André-Charles Boulle for a pendule longue ligne, described as a 'Pendule à secondes'

matched that of the clock itself. When French ébénistes produced long-case clocks they were known as pendules longue lignes and they resembled an arch-topped type of bracket clock on a lyre-shaped tall case, richly elaborated with gilded bronze mounts fitted to the wooden veneered carcase, with a glazed lenticle, or small window, to view the pendulum bob. André-Charles Boulle certainly designed such clocks, and one of his drawings is illustrated here inscribed 'Grande Pendule à Secondes', but it is so fanciful that perhaps it was never made. The extravagance of French clock styles is often misunderstood by English writers, but it must be remembered that they were intended as integral features of galleries and salons in the palaces and houses of the rich, and were not to be judged in isolation, as objects separate from tables, chairs, mirrors, candelabra, chimneypieces, plasterwork and other elements of the interior design of the day. It would, indeed, be true to say that French taste, at least in a domestic sense, has always regarded the clock as more of a work of art than as a scientific instrument, though this is in no way to suggest that French horologists were not men of the finest scientific calibre, just as skilful as their English contemporaries, and sometimes more enterprising.

To turn from the extravagance of French taste to the more restrained clocks of English design is to witness a development which is not in the mainstream of French-inspired high Baroque, to which the 'Mostyn' Tompion belongs, but rather it has a quieter domestic quality which is rich too, in its own way, but very different. The prevailing influence on English clocks of the late 17th century, where it exists at all, is Dutch rather than French, but international Baroque is still quietly present in some case ornaments, in architectural mouldings and in dial spandrel mounts. The domestic clock begins to reach a far wider range of households than had ever been possible before.

The technique of decorating the case of a clock in marquetry quickly spread to England in the last quarter of the 17th century, though unlike the French Boulle marquetry style metal was not used in the veneered designs, but simply timbers of contrasting colours and tones, and of elegant figure. English marquetry is predominantly Dutch in inspiration, and a fine example of an English veneered longcase clock datable to about 1680 is one by Joseph Knibb (1640–1711), a clock which was formerly in the famous Wetherfield collection which was dispersed in 1928. Its slender proportioned oak case has the main trunk door covered with symmetrically arranged walnut 'oyster shell' veneers, so-called because the timber was cut in fine slices from across the bough, giving the general appearance of pairs of oyster shells. Within this ground are two oval roundels on the door with a further roundel on the plinth, each oval reserve being veneered with a black ebony ground and elaborate arrangements of flowers, leaves, vases and birds in different coloured woods and green stained bone or ivory. Features to note in cases such as this are the half-round cock beading, veneered across the curve, to hide the gap between the door edge and the case; the convex moulding below the hood; the glazed aperture or lenticle through which the pendulum bob was seen; and the twist-turned three-quarter columns on each side of the hood door. The style of this kind of twist turning, extensively used on other pieces of furniture of the period, is traceable to Italian architecture, having become a basic early feature of Baroque design, especially in Bernini's first masterpiece of Baroque decoration, the enormous baldacchino on twisted columns in St Peter's, Rome. Another example of the feature may be seen at St Mary the Virgin, Oxford, in the portico designed in 1637 by Nicholas Stone. As Joseph Knibb fitted an anchor escapement to the turret clock at St Mary's in

Longcase clock with an 'oyster-shell' marquetry veneered case; twist-turned three-quarter columns on hood but cresting missing; signed Joseph Knibb, London; about 1680. *Museum and Art Gallery, Salford*

1669–70 and was resident in Oxford from about 1662 to 1670, he must have known this portico well. It is a matter of some conjecture as to whether or not the flat tops of the hoods of clocks such as the Joseph Knibb were originally left as a straight top line, or whether they formerly had a carved cresting. Cresting was certainly used though few survive complete today, but another clock by Joseph Knibb is shown with its cresting intact.

The fashion for marquetry in fine quality clock cases continued until the early years of the 18th century, but not in the same vigorous and attractively naïve manner. By 1700 a much more detailed and elaborate form had evolved which is known as arabesque marquetry, far more in keeping with the French Baroque style of Boulle. A detailed view of a longcase clock by Peter Garon of London shows a finely detailed overall type of design incorporating leaves, flowers, vases and birds. These elements are linked together on an ebony ground with symmetrically scrolled leaves, reminding us of Jean Tijou's screen at Hampton Court. Not content with this arabesque marquetry on the main trunk door only, it spread its network over the whole case and mouldings. Such continuous and intricate work is sometimes known as seaweed marquetry, or even endive (a species of chicory with curved leaves) and the designer who is thought to have introduced this fashion in English furniture was Gerreit Jensen (known in England as Garrett Johnson), who, significantly enough, also introduced Boulle-type work using brass, tortoiseshell and pewter, but not in clock cases. The finely worked seaweed or endive marquetry was the last use of marquetry at

Longcase clock in ebony with its original cresting on the hood; twist-turned three-quarter columns and skeleton dial; signed Joseph Knibb, London; about 1685. *Fitzwilliam Museum, Cambridge*

all in English longcase clocks, apart from certain revivals at a later date, for fashion changed to plain walnut and ultimately mahogany.

Longcase clock dials of the Baroque period in England must be noted in some detail, for like other aspects of the casework they were not simply new ideas, but took their style from traditions of the past and prevailing architectural taste. A characteristic feature which is found in almost all longcase clock dials from their beginning in the 1660s until the end of the longcase period, at the end of the 18th century, is the applied relief mount in each corner of the dial, known as a spandrel.

The earliest forms of spandrel consisted of a cherub's head with a pair of outstretched wings, the earliest types generally being small against the dial back plate, but later gradually increasing in size until almost the complete corner between the chapter ring and the edge of the dial was filled. By the end of the 17th century a number of scrolled leaves had been added to the basic winged cherub's head, while another popular shape was introduced in the form of winged cherubs supporting a crown. Winged cherubs' heads have already been noted as a Baroque feature in the reference to the base of Tompion's three-month clock for William III. Cherubs, sometimes referred to as putti or even cupids are an interesting intermixture of Christian symbolism and Roman pagan ideas. 'Cherub' means an angelic being gifted with knowledge and love, while 'cupid' is a beautiful young boy, also symbolic of love but in a physical rather than a spiritual sense. Thus we see Baroque European art using classical pagan forms re-interpreted in a Western Christian world. Roman art abounds with winged cupids, as does the Mannerist art of 16th-century Italy, for example in the work of artists such as Andrea della Robbia, whose 'Adoration' relief panel in terra-cotta combines the Virgin Mary adoring the Christ child with a pair of winged cupids looking on from above. By the Mannerist and Baroque routes the winged cupids' heads came into English decorative art of the 16th and 17th centuries, in scores of church monuments, often as complete amorini (the full winged figure of a child), in painting, in silver plate, in architectural sculpture such as Grinling Gibbons' canopy of the Bishop's throne at St Paul's Cathedral and in countless other places. Little wonder, therefore, that it was adopted as a device in the decoration of clock dials, in its later phases incorporating the Royal Crown, perhaps to emulate a similar profusion of cherubs on the French clocks of 'le Roi Soleil'—the sun-king Louis XIV.

The dials of longcase clocks, like their smaller brothers, the spring-driven bracket clocks, had evolved from the early Renaissance styles. By the later years of the 17th century they consisted of a dial plate of brass, a silvered chapter ring with engraved numerals filled with black wax, a set of four cast and gilded spandrel mounts at the corners, a separate silvered dial inside the chapter ring for the seconds, a pair of plain winding holes at first, but later, and surviving until about 1725, accentuated with ringed mouldings, and a plain matted main dial centre enlivened only with engraved patterns round the square calendar aperture. Minor changes were introduced as the years passed, but a good example of a dial of between 1700 and 1710 may be seen in the one signed by John Knapp of Reading. An almost exactly similar dial from a clock by a Nantwich maker raises the question as to how it could be that two dials, by two different makers 150 miles apart, could be so similar, with virtually identical use of three engraved crowns above the calendar square? The obvious answer is that dialmaking was a specialised trade, the majority of its craftsmen working in London at this date from whom dials could be acquired both in the capital city and in the provinces alike. The evolution of dials in a more or less standardised

Detail of arabesque marquetry on the door of a longcase clock by Peter Garon, London; about 1700. *City Art Gallery, Manchester*

Opposite page (right)
Portico of the Church of St Mary the Virgin, Oxford; designed by Nicholas Stone in 1637

way suggests that this was the way in which much of the clock trade was structured, for dialmaking, movement-making and casemaking were quite different activities which only came together through the retailing arrangements of the complete clock 'maker', whose name appeared in a prominent place. That the Tompions, Knibbs, and others produced and retailed clocks of outstanding quality is only to underline that they were extremely careful in their choice of dial, movement and casemakers. They imposed their standards of design, quality and craftsmanship on their sub-contractors, and they were acutely aware of the importance of providing quality products at high prices for a London-based (and sometimes international) upper class and aristocratic clientèle.

Before leaving the subject of longcase clock dials a particular type of dial must be mentioned which indicates most clearly the increasing perfection and accuracy of 17th and early 18th century clockmaking. Of many which might have been chosen a superb, year-going clock signed by Daniel Quare (1649–1724) in the British Museum has a subsidiary dial to indicate the 'equation of time'. During a complete year the apparent time as indicated by a sundial does not coincide with what is known as 'mean time', ie the 24 hours of a mean solar day, each day being of exactly the same length. Because of the variation from a true

Below left
Silver-gilt cup and cover, hallmarked London 1573–4; known as the Magdalen Cup this shows an early use in England of the winged cherub's head in its decoration. *City Art Gallery, Manchester*

Below right
Gravestone in the churchyard at Beaminster, Dorset, illustrating the popular use of the winged cherub's head; 1716

Above left
Dial of a longcase clock showing winged cherub's head spandrels; signed John Knapp, Reading; 1700–10

Above right
Dial of a longcase clock almost identical to that of John Knapp of Reading, but this one signed Tho. Talbott, Namptwich; 1700–10

circle of the orbit of the Earth round the Sun, and also because of the inclination of the Earth's axis to the ecliptic (the plane of the Earth's orbit) the time as read by a sundial shows that on only four days each year are 'solar' days and 'mean' days the same length, these dates being about 16 April, 14 June, 1 September and 25 December. Between these dates the deviation may be up to 16 minutes, though this deviation is not at a constant rate of 'too fast' or 'too slow'. From the 21 to 24 October the reading of a clock against a sundial will show that the clock is 16 minutes too 'slow' if it is running to true mean time, and almost 15 minutes too 'fast' at the end of January and the beginning of February. A recently discovered label pasted behind the door of a Daniel Quare longcase clock sets out in detail, for each day of the year, the amount of deviation between the readings of a sundial and mean time, to enable the owner of the clock to set it accurately after consulting the sundial. This is a salutary reminder today that the use of a common sundial was the only way, 300 years ago, by which a clock could be set and its timekeeping checked.

To return to the British Museum Daniel Quare year clock the illustration shows that there is a subsidiary dial which appears through a glazed aperture in the upper trunk door. This dial, driven from the main clockwork, indicates automatically the equation of time for every day of the year, and there is evidence to show that this part of the clock was not made in Quare's workshop, but by a man called Joseph Williamson (1669?–1725), a mathematician with knowledge of astronomy who claimed to have made all the equation dials used in English clocks up to 1719. Equation clocks, as they are called, were popular with the most outstanding makers of the day, but the invention of the kidney-shaped cam, which made the whole operation possible, was yet one more of the inventions of Christiaan Huygens.

Of several equation clocks made by Thomas Tompion, one of the best-known examples was made by him for the Pump Room in Bath. In his later years Tompion, in a declining state of health, like many well-to-do citizens of his day visited Bath to take the waters. It would appear that he stayed there for quite long periods and in 1707 he was made an Honorary Freeman of the city. Presumably in return for this honour he gave, in 1709, a month-going equation clock to be installed in

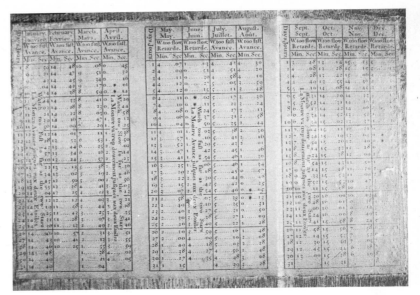

Right
An equation table pasted inside the trunk door of a Daniel Quare longcase clock

Below
Year-going longcase clock with equation dial in the veneered trunk door; gilded bronze mounts with scrolled feet and Baroque ornament at the base; signed Daniel Quare, London; about 1710.
British Museum, London

the new Pump Room which was erected in 1706. The equation clock (see p. 67) is still there today, but not in the same Pump Room, for this was re-built in the 1790s. Its 9 ft (274 cm) high case, made of oak, was designed in the form of a single Roman Tuscan column, half-round in section against a rectangular trunk but giving the visual impression of supporting the square hood which has a segmental arch above. In true Baroque manner the front corners of the hood are decorated with herms, a feature in which a male head is fully carved but the rest of the figure is a plain, quadrangular column tapering downwards. These decorative herms may be traced back to Greek times when the Greek god Hermes (called Mercury by the Romans) was the subject of many carved heads on tapering columns in the streets of ancient Athens. The dial of the clock has an arch above it which contains an aperture to reveal the date and month, and a hand which indicates, on an outer scale, the minutes by which the Sun will be faster or slower at noon than mean time for the date shown. This arched dial top, known as a break-arch, became a normal feature of longcase clocks by about 1720 and Tompion's use of it here must be considered as one of the earliest examples known.

To have used an equation clock efficiently it is obvious that a sundial was a *sine qua non*, and Tompion provided the City of Bath with a sundial to use with his clock. This sundial appears to have been in regular use, perhaps until the Pump Room re-building at the end of the 18th century, but eventually it vanished from the scene. By great good fortune it was later found in a dump of nettles on a farm at Corsham, Wiltshire in a corroded state but with its original engraving of hour scale and signature still quite clear. After careful restoration the sundial was set up, on a new pillar, and on 6 July 1971 was unveiled by the Astronomer Royal, Sir Richard Woolley and formally handed back to the Mayor of Bath.

Tompion's Bath clock is a fine and noble Baroque masterpiece, and fitting that it should be one of his last productions, for he died on 20 November 1713. His place of burial may still be seen in Westminster Abbey in the same grave as his equally famous clockmaking partner, friend and husband of his niece, George Graham (b 1673), who followed him there in 1751. Burial in Westminster Abbey in the 18th century was reserved for those of the nobility and gentry who could afford the fees due to the Dean, and Tompion's reputation and success in commercial life had clearly made him eligible. From the quality of the clocks which he has left behind, and from hints that he was an inventor in his own right as well as a maker of new devices designed by Robert Hooke and others, it is clear that he was a man of taste, of extraordinary skill and also having considerable business acumen.

We must now turn to a final aspect of clock case design of the Baroque period which, in a sense and in spirit belongs more closely to the era of Rococo fantasy of the 18th century, but yet was born as a European fashion in the 17th century. The style in question is that of lacquered furniture, which takes us back to the Orient and to the factors which led to the use of lacquer decoration in clocks.

Of the various extravagances of furnishing styles of the late 17th century the fashion for lacquer was perhaps the most bizarre. Known in the 17th century as 'Indian' taste (as a result of a very vague understanding of oriental geography by most Europeans), the importation of oriental goods and artefacts had already begun, on a small scale, in the 16th century, when the first examples of Chinese porcelain began to filter to the West. Direct trade between Europe and China began in 1517

Sundial originally erected at the Pump Room, Bath; made by Thomas Tompion to accompany his equation clock. This sundial became lost but was rediscovered and restored in 1971. *Bath Museums Service*

Watercolour painting by Humphrey Repton of the interior of the Pump Room, Bath, showing Tompion's clock on the rear wall; dated 1784. *Bath Museums Service*

when Manuel I of Portugal established an embassy in Peking, the first imports resulting from this link being porcelain, or 'china' as it was called. Further ventures eventually led to the formation of the English East India Company in 1600 and its Dutch counterpart, the Vereenigde Oestindische Compagnie in 1602. At first oriental spices as well as ceramics were the main reason for the trade, but examples of Chinese and Japanese lacquered objects also came to Europe with tea, chintzes and other exotic articles of eastern style. In 1598 Van Linschoten wrote this account of lacquer from his voyage to the East Indies: 'the fayrest workemanshippe thereof cometh from China, as may be seene by all things that come from thence, as desks, Targets, Tables, Cubbordes, Boxes and a thousand such like things, that are all covered and wrought with Lac of all colours and fashions'. England, Holland and France became the major importers of oriental objects, and the fashion for oriental lacquer really took hold in the latter part of the 17th century, during the English Restoration and the period of Louis XIV. There are two basic types of lacquer decoration, one being very hard and durable produced with endless patience from successive coats of natural resin-

Longcase clock in a black japanned case with its original decoration intact; the upper dial is unusual, having the calendar indication in an arch, re-set by pulling a cord at the end of each month; signed John Jordan, London; about 1720–25. *Courtesy of Strike One (Islington) Limited, London*

ous sap from lacquer trees, and the other a more highly polished surface with decoration in relief, usually known as 'Japan' work. Both styles of lacquer came to Europe in the form of large screens, table tops, panels, frames, etc. and a popular use of such items was to cut them up to make other furniture. So great was the demand for lacquered work that European substitutes quickly appeared, inferior to the true oriental work and usually of the 'raised' or Japan style. Complete items of European joinery, or detachable parts such as cabinet doors, were sent to China for lacquering and the Chinese themselves quickly recognised the importance of this trade and made articles of furniture for export in a lacquered finish. So fast was the rise in popularity of lacquered designs that a 'do-it-yourself' textbook was published in 1688 by John Stalker and George Parker entitled *Treatise of Japanning and Varnishing, Being a Compleat Discovery of those Arts: With the best way of making all sorts of Varnish for Japan . . .*, and books such as this stimulated the craze for this 'make believe' world. It is no coincidence that the same period saw the introduction to Europe of tea and coffee drinking, and the making and importation of the furniture appropriate to this new fashion.

As a new item of furniture it is not surprising that the longcase clock, and to some extent the bracket clock, became an object for decoration with lacquer. Virtually all lacquered clock cases are of European japanned technique since the problem of sending parts of cases such as the trunk door to the Far East took so long, a period of not less than three years. Japanned clock cases are also of the more popular 'raised' japan type in which salient features of the Chinese inspired designs, especially on the doors and sometimes on the plinths, were built up on a gesso ground (made from glue size and whitening) which was varnished to a high gloss with the raised portions gilded and/or coloured. The plain areas of the trunk sides and hood were left flat and simply coloured or gilded with patterns mostly, but sometimes pictorial designs on oriental themes. The flat ground of the japanning was usually black, but occasionally a rich red or a deep green might be used. The inferior quality of most English japanned clock cases was such that most are now but a dim reflection of what they must have been when new, and they cannot stand comparison with true oriental work which may more often be seen in 17th-century cabinets on Baroque carved and gilded stands. Unlike natural timbers, which with their polish, patina, colour and grain have improved with age, the artificial lacquer on oak for the best clocks and pine for the inferior, has now become dull and worn, and it has also a regrettable tendency to crack and flake.

Japanned clock cases continued in vogue until well into the 18th century, and the exotic, romantic, eccentric and even fantastic nature of their style takes us naturally into the world of Rococo, which is the subject of the following chapter.

Leaving behind the extravagant world of 17th-century furnishing, with its elaborate Baroque pomp, let us finish with a homely note from a northern English country squire, Nicholas Blundell, who lived on his farm near the Lancashire coast, and kept a daily diary or *Great Diurnal* as he called it. On 10 August 1709 he 'put a new Clock-Cord to the Pendulum' and on 5 December in the same year 'took the Larum Pendulum in peeses and clensed it'. In 1710, on 28 September, he records: 'I took the Little Pendelum in our Chamber in peeses and dressed it', by which he presumably meant that he cleaned out the dirt and re-oiled it. By Nicholas Blundell's time the 'larum pendelum' and the chamber clock were common possessions of the yeoman farming and merchant class, and were not the sole prerogative of the wealthy and the great.

EUROPEAN ROCOCO
Fantasy and Precision

In complete contrast to the heavy ornament and architectural weight of Baroque, the 18th century in Europe saw the evolution and flowering of a new style of decoration and furniture design which is known by the name of Rococo. As far as England is concerned the style should rightly be called a 'fashion', for it was imported from France and had a limited vogue, from about 1735 until the 1770s when it was replaced by the cool and restrained lines of Neo-Classicism. Unlike the Baroque, Rococo is largely concerned with interior design, incorporating furniture, plasterwork, textiles, fireplaces, carpets and the like, whilst the exterior architectural style of buildings continued in a traditional classical way, in England especially, as a revival of Inigo Jones's Palladianism of the 17th century. Early in the 18th century architects such as William Kent (1685–1748) and his patron Richard Boyle (1694–1753), otherwise known as Lord Burlington, sought to re-discover the purity of the Roman classical style in reaction to the excesses of the Baroque. English architects following them developed a vernacular style of domestic building of impeccable proportions and taste, generally, if rather vaguely, referred to as Georgian. Clock cases, as part of Georgian domestic furnishing also followed on classical lines of Palladian inspiration, in veneered walnut until about 1750 and later in mahogany, but the Rococo vogue, imported from outside, had a considerable influence.

To define the meaning of the word Rococo it is necessary to look at its French source, and to recognise that in France the style had gradually evolved through the elaborate designs of Boulle, away from the structural and formal manner to an expression of free-flowing, asymmetrical, convoluted, double-scrolled curves which took the eye away from the tectonic, or structural, to the organic and naturalistic. Its first great exponent was the cabinetmaker Charles Cressent (1685–1768) who enlivened with curves and bright gay colours the massive style of Boulle. By 1730 the new vogue was taken up with enthusiasm by the Italian-born Juste-Aurèle Meissonnier (1695–1750) and the Dutch architect Gilles Marie Oppenord (1672–1742). Described by the great French horological historian Tardy (Henri-Gustave-Eugène Lengellé—1901–71) as 'delicate, alive, seductive, gallant, licentious, dissolute, but always graceful or courteous' is perhaps to use French exaggeration which itself might be called Rococo, but these words sum up a French characteristic, and Rococo is characteristically French.

A drawing by an unknown designer in the Musée des Arts Decoratifs in Paris, not for a clock but for an epergne or table-candlestand, expresses admirably the spirit of Rococo. Not a single straight line of architectural construction appears in the drawing. The epergne was intended to be made in silver or bronze as a fantastic assembly of 'C' and 'S' scrolls, writhing and flowing, partly asymmetrical where it supports the figure of Bacchus being offered a bowl of fruit by a winged cupid; gently supporting the two goddesses Flora and Ceres on the left and right respectively, seated on double-scrolled arms. Floral fronds support the candles from which grow flowing leaves, and the whole design is an extraordinary figment of creative imagery. It may not be to everyone's taste, for this must be acquired. Rococo is not concerned with reason, but rather with emotive fantasy and frivolous joy.

French clocks of the Rococo period are mostly referred to as pendules Louis XV from the coincidence of Rococo with the years of that king's reign (1723–74), and they are of immense variety. In general terms they can be divided into four main types, the bracket clock permanently standing on its matching bracket which is secured to a wall; the cartel clock which is suspended directly from the wall; the mantel clock which is normally found on a fireplace overmantel, or table clock of the same shape but placed on a sidetable which usually has a marble top; and the régulateur or longcase clock, or pendule longue ligne, which is something of a rarity in France. As well as being created in a variety of superlatively styled cases, French clocks of the period also saw the introduction of porcelain and marble as materials of their general construction and decoration, and at a later stage they were entirely made of metal. For those clocks made in wood exquisitely selected veneers continued to be used, with Boulle-type marquetry surviving until about 1750. The use of a new type of japanning known as vernis Martin was important too, both veneered and japanned cases being fitted with numerous gilded cast bronze mounts which became a dominant feature of French furniture design, quite apart from clocks.

To emphasise a point made earlier, that French clock cases were considered as works of art, the names of the ébénistes or cabinetmakers are often to be found on superlative cases of Rococo design. A régulateur at Waddesdon Manor has the name of its maker Jean Pierre Latz (*c* 1691–1754) stamped on the back, and this is a good example of an oak cased clock, veneered in mahogany, kingwood and purplewood, of undulating form, copiously mounted with gilded bronzes in 'C' and 'S' scrolls. Even more elaborate with its swirling scrolls, grotesque mask, branching candelabra, exotic birds on each side of the lenticle, and tremendous lion's claw feet, is the drawing for a régulateur by Juste-Aurèle Meissonnier which survives in the French National Archives. Far more common, but equally alive with Rococo scrolls and devices, was the wall-mounted bracket clock such as the 18th-century example with a 19th-century movement signed Chatenay à Versailles (see p. 67). This may be seen at the Bowes Museum, Co. Durham, a museum favoured by much French art. Its treatment reminds one of the tapestry panels at Newby Hall, Yorkshire, woven at the Gobelins royal factory in 1769, after designs by the painter François Boucher, depicting the loves of the gods. Though a little later than the Chatenay clock case they echo the charm and fantasy of the Rococo world. Just as the tapestries are bedecked with flowers, so the bracket clock has flowers painted too, between the gilded mounts on the body of the case, but in the new technique of vernis Martin.

In a manner not unlike that used for the decoration of English lacquered clocks vernis Martin was a development of varnishes and lacquers to imitate Chinese and Japanese work, for which the Martin family became justly famous. The four Martin brothers, Guillaume, Étienne-Simon, Julien and Robert, established their workshops in Paris which were dignified by the name of 'manufactures royales' in 1749, and as well as using oriental designs they also worked in naturalistic flowers and leaves on coloured grounds, mostly green or red, but of other colours too. It is the quality and contrast and vivid sense of movement of the gilded metal mounts against the lacquered ground which gives vernis Martin its richness and colourful charm, unlike the now often fading lacquer of English longcase clocks with inferior gilding and little sense of relief.

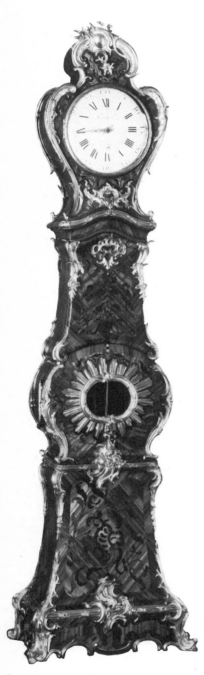

French longcase clock or régulateur, veneered and decorated with gilded bronze mounts; enamelled dial; the movement is signed Cronier à Paris and the case is stamped Jean-Pierre Latz; about 1750. *National Trust, Waddesdon Manor, Bucks*

The richness and quality of French gilded bronzes of the period Louis XV is quite unsurpassed in extravagance and skill. By 1750 to the end of the century, and beyond, many clock cases were either entirely of bronze or having wooden carcases elaborated with metal, the contrasts necessary for richness of effect coming from silk fabrics or the addition of porcelain details. A metal-cased mantel clock of superlative quality is in the Wallace Collection in London, signed by François Viger. The richly ornamental yet vigorously convoluted scrolls terminating in acanthus leaves or 'celery' leaves, with flowers too, are most carefully cast and later filed, chiselled, chased and burnished to provide a superbly detailed finish for gilding. A dog and defeated eagle crown the top with a horn and other musical trophies below. Mantel clocks such as the Viger were often placed in front of mirrors, either on a mantelpiece or side table, the mirrors being known as pier glasses when fitted between windows, and they were very popular in French interiors. Since the backs of mantel or table clocks were therefore frequently seen in reflection, the backs were carefully finished too.

The dog on the Viger clock is a reminder of another group of extravagant French mantel clocks in which animals were frequently a major part of the design. Elephants, bulls, horses, lions, rhinoceroses and other quadrupeds are often to be found, in patinated bronze, with the main clock case and other features on their backs, and sometimes human figures, either western or oriental, were part of the design in the same kind of way. This love of animal and human forms to decorate clocks in the 18th century was very much a part of the universal spirit of Rococo, an urge which stimulated the porcelain makers of Meissen, Nymphenburg, Frankenthal, Vincennes, Chelsea, Bow and many other European factories to model superb miniature figures and figure groups with which to decorate mantelpieces, tables and porcelain display cabinets.

The importation of porcelain from the Far East in the 17th century has already been noticed. The secret of making fine oriental porcelain was eagerly sought by European potters from the 17th century onwards because this new material, hard, translucent and glowing white, had captured the imagination of creative potters and collectors alike. The first ceramist to unravel the secrets of this material and provide a western-based manufacture to satisfy this aspect of the craze known as

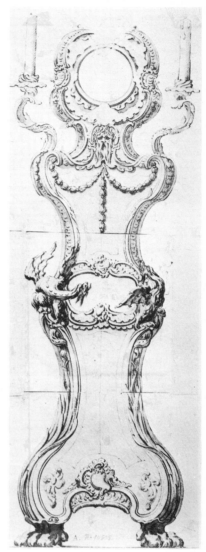

Drawing for an elaborate régulateur by Juste-Aurèle Meissonnier; mid-18th century

Design for an epergne or surtout-de-table in the Rococo manner; mid-18th century

'Chinamania' was Johann Friedrich Böttger (1682–1719), who had been appointed by Augustus the Strong, Elector of Saxony and King of Poland to undertake experiments to turn base metals into gold. Having inevitably failed in this task his work with refractory materials had given him an insight into their behaviour under intense heat, and in due course, working with Ehrenfried Walther von Tschirnhausen he produced a fine white porcelain from Kolditz clay in 1708. With this discovery of porcelain, of the true Chinese hard-paste type, a factory was founded at Meissen in 1710 to produce elegant tablewares and ornamental figures, decorated in coloured enamels, employing such famous artists as the modeller Johann Joachim Kändler and the painter Christian Friedrich Heröldt. The charming, delicate, fragile and yet at the same time strong nature of the new material epitomised the spirit of Rococo completely and it was extensively used not only for tablewares but for decorative figures, candlestands, trinket boxes and countless other frivolities of aristocratic taste. By the middle of the 18th century china-making factories in addition to Meissen had been established in Germany at Nymphenburg, Frankenthal, Fürstenburg, Berlin and several other places, while in France St Cloud, Chantilly and Vincennes were also engaged in this delicate art.

The clock casemakers of the Rococo period were quick to sense how appropriate porcelain could be to capture the spirit of the style, and by the 1750s mantel and table clock cases were being produced with floral bocages and figures in china. Command of the new materials was not yet sufficiently advanced to attempt to make complete cases in porcelain, but fitted to a metal frame or stand the china figures and other decorative devices formed a marvellous contrast with the gilded metal and introduced a delicacy of finish not attainable in any other way. A splendid clock case from Waddesdon Manor is composed of branches and leaves in gilded bronze with porcelain flowers added, from the factory at Vincennes, while the base of the clock has a set of the famous Meissen monkey musicians originally modelled by Kändler and said to have been designed as a satire on the Dresden Court Orchestra. Porcelain mounted mantel clocks of this type, like the example from Brodick Castle in the Isle of Arran, were accompanied by a flanking pair of candelabra to produce a 'matching set' or garniture de cheminée as they are frequently called, a vogue which became particularly popular in the later part of the century.

Clockmaking in France in the 18th century had become so thriving a trade, and the clock itself so important a focal point in the lavish interiors of other fine furniture and fittings, that their range of styles and design within basic categories is almost endless. Yet another form is the cartel clock, a wall-hanging clock covered with elaborately moulded bronze mounts in much the same way as mantel and table clocks, but often even more elaborate in their form. Such a clock is the example by Julien le Roy in the J. Paul Getty Museum in California. Julien le Roy (1686–1759) was one of the most notable makers in France in his day and became one of the few privileged *Horlogers du Roy* who were given special status by the king, who attended to the clocks in the royal palace at Versailles and who were given free apartments in the Louvre in Paris. Such men were not restricted by the limitations imposed by the guilds which defined the areas of clockmaking into movement-making, casemaking, dialmaking and bronze mount-casting as quite separate spheres of responsibility, not to be trespassed upon by workers in the other sections. In this cartel clock Julien le Roy's movement is fitted in a single-piece bronze casting by the celebrated casemaker Jacques Caffieri, only the figure of Minerva above, a branch of oak leaves and

Opposite page
(*above left*) French musical mantel clock of gilded bronze, crowned with a dog and prostrate eagle; musical instruments below on the sumptuous metal casework; signed François Viger; mid-18th century. *Wallace Collection, London*
(*above right*) French clock and musical box decorated with a set of Meissen porcelain monkey musicians and Vincennes porcelain flowers; the clock movement is a 19th-century replacement; about 1755. *National Trust, Waddesdon Manor, Bucks*
(*below*) French 'garniture de cheminée'; the clock case and candle-holders are of gilded bronze, the figures of Meissen porcelain and the flowers of soft-paste French porcelain. Made about 1755, but the movement a later replacement. *Brodick Castle, Isle of Arran, Courtesy of the National Trust for Scotland*

Below
French cartel clock (wall clock) made entirely of gilded bronze, incorporating Minerva and Cupid in its Rococo design; movement signed Julien le Roy (Paris), case stamped Jacques Caffieri; about 1748. *J. Paul Getty Museum, Malibu, California*

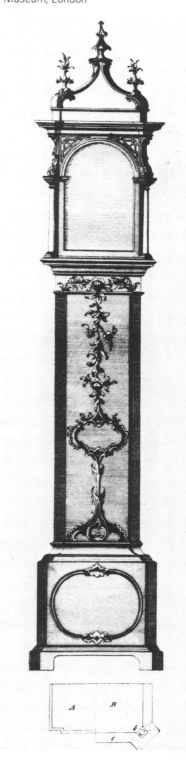

Below
Design for a longcase clock from Plate 135 of Thomas Chippendale's *The Gentleman and Cabinet-Maker's Director*, 1754. *Victoria and Albert Museum, London*

Hood and dial of a Dutch pedestal organ clock; the carved wooden cabinet is fitted with gilded bronze grilles and the dial plate is painted; signed J. George Gruning, Amsterdam; about 1750. *Lady Lever Art Gallery, Port Sunlight*

Opposite page
Drop-front secrétaire mounted with a clock which has two dials, the lower concealed when the desk is closed; gilded mounts and lacquer decoration; stamped I. Dubois and J. Goyer; about 1770. *National Trust, Waddesdon Manor, Bucks*

Bracket clock with repeat striking in an ebonised case with break-arch dial; signed John Everell, London; about 1745. *Stuart Hall Collection*

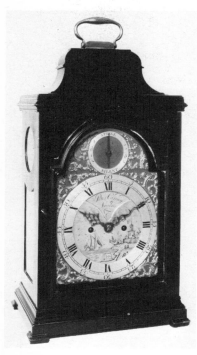

Bracket clock with conventional striking in an ebonised case with break-arch dial engraved with a maritime scene; signed Peter Carney, London; about 1775

the winged cherub on the left being separately made and attached as independent castings.

Before leaving French clocks in the Rococo manner, notice must be taken of yet one more type in which the clock has become but a part in another piece of furniture. The fitting of clocks to tables, cabinets and desks was just coming into fashion in the middle of the 18th century, an idea which increased as the century drew to its close. A drop-front desk from Waddesdon Manor has two clock dials, one above the cabinet itself and the other inside, the whole piece being elaborated with gilt classical mounts, and with lacquer in the Chinese style. A final French Rococo masterpiece from the Wallace Collection in London is the enormous and superlative clock invented by Alexandre Fortier for Michel Stollewerk—an unusual 'tour de force' of sumptuous cabinet-work and mechanical ingenuity (see p. 68). On its four dials it indicates solar and mean time, the phases of the Moon, and a complex indication of planetary motions.

From the imaginative and extraordinary world of French Rococo clockmaking we must now move to England where Rococo flourished, but in a more modest way. Another grand clock on the scale of the Stollewerk but of English fabrication is a large organ clock at Temple Newsam in Leeds (see p. 102). This immense masterpiece by George Pyke of London is in essence a pedestal clock, the upper cabinet standing on a heavy matching plinth, hollow to accommodate the enormous weight which powers the organ bellows and barrel, made in 1765. The quality and feeling of Rococo is expressed in the fact that it is an organ and automata clock, playing its tunes (if required) every three hours, having a painted dial representing a landscape with ornamental bridge, harbour, and sea behind, a fortified tower and watermill with wheel complete, and a group of people dancing as if on the terrace of a country house. When the clock strikes and the organ plays many of the figures move; a dog chases a duck, the musicians play their fiddles, the waterwheel turns and sailing ships cross the estuary through moving waves. Here is the magical, fanciful, irrelevant conceit of pleasure and fun, having no relationship to the clock's main purpose to show the time, of especial attraction 200 years before the world was inundated with a plethora of visual imagery. The architectural form of its case expresses, perhaps, more of the character of sturdy Baroque with its Roman Composite columns, its semi-circular arched front and sides and its pierced symmetrical grilles through which the sound of the organ may be heard; but the relief gilded mounts above and below the dial, its figure of Mercury or Eros on top and particularly its gilded bronze relief in front of the painted dial, depicting the seven Muses and Diana and Apollo on plinths at the sides, posed with theatrical nonchalance, is pure Rococo. Once could almost believe that the clock was made in France, for the white enamel dial is typically French in style, not following at all the English tradition.

A similar majestic clock, but this time Dutch and by J. George Gruning of Amsterdam, is in the Lady Lever Art Gallery at Port Sunlight, and it has a similar painted dial but no moving automata figures. The dial is a curious combination of the traditional silvered chapter ring on a matted brass plate, but surrounded by a painted background to make the dial appear as if part of a Rococo styled mantel clock. The painting is by Jacobus Buys who placed a youthful female figure (life) on the left of the painted clock, and the figure of Father Time (death) on the right. Above them, in the clouds, four winged cherubs symbolise music, the arts and science. Like the George Pyke clock, this massive and superb piece of about 1750 retains strong elements of

Above
French clock with matching bracket, decorated with flowers in Vernis Martin; 19th-century movement; signed Chatenay à Versailles; about 1750. *The Bowes Museum, Barnard Castle, Co. Durham*

Left
Month-going equation clock made by Thomas Tompion for the Pump Room, Bath; the trunk of the case is in the form of a Roman Tuscan column; break-arch dial with a pair of herms on the corners of the hood; made by Tompion for the Pump Room in 1709. *Bath Museums Service*

Baroque, intermixed with Rococo details such as the pierced and gilded grilles at the sides, for the architectural solidity of earlier years held the stage far longer in England and Holland than it did in France.

In English design, Rococo flourished from about 1740 until the 1770s, but rarely with full-blooded vigour as in France, as far as clocks were concerned. One of the reasons why styles of design began to spread through Europe more quickly than ever before was the influence of pattern books put out for the furnishing trades, for cabinetmakers and retailing agents. The international intention of these publications is illustrated by the fact that the cabinetmakers William Ince and John Mayhew published their *The Universal System of Household Furniture* in 1762 with the title page and part of the text in French as well as in English. A more famous book, Thomas Chippendale's *The Gentleman and Cabinet-Maker's Director*, first published in 1754, came out in a French edition in 1762 under the title of *Le Guide du Tapissier, de l'Ébéniste et de tous ceux qui travaillent en meubles . . . troisième édition . . . Londres*. This mammoth folio of 161 plates has a few examples of clock case designs, one of which is illustrated on page 65. If this is compared with a French mantel clock and régulateur, the cool architectural lines of Chippendale's design are obvious, for the floral scrolls and leaves and the double-scrolled pagoda-like top are the only Rococo forms on this otherwise restrained design.

The illustration mentioned above is a good example of the proposed use of Rococo motifs on English clocks, but even this amount of the style is rare to find in an actual example, where generally speaking the French influence is mainly restricted to the dial itself, with perhaps a few flourishes here and there on a case which will otherwise be rendered in dignified classical style. To illustrate this point two English bracket clocks will be compared, one made before the onset of Rococo fashions and the other in which the style has made itself felt. The first clock is a single train, repeat striking clock by John Everell of London, made about 1745, and the other is a two-train striking clock by Peter Carney, also of London, made in the 1770s. A common feature shared by both is the break-arch dial which first appeared in English domestic clocks about 1715–20, and they are also both housed in ebonised cases, with carrying handles for moving them about. The differences, however, will show how the dictates of fashion gradually make their mark as the years go by. The first important feature which is different in these cases is the shape of the top, the earlier Everell being of an inverted bell shape, with ovolo moulding below and cavetto moulding above, whereas the Carney clock has a true bell top with the convex or ovolo moulding above the cavetto or concave. The visual effect of this subtle change is to make the former clock look more squat and square, while the latter gains height and emphasis on its narrower form. The handles too are different, the earlier being square in section and centrally turned with architectural mouldings like a baluster on its side, which links it more closely with Baroque, while the Carney clock has a simple modelled curve to grip in the hand, of organic rather than tectonic form. The dials of these clocks are quite different in treatment. The earlier has heavy scrolled mask spandrels, a chapter ring with half-hour divisions, quarter-hour marking on the inner edge (a relic of single-handed clocks), a matted centre dial with 'mock' pendulum aperture and date aperture above, and its maker's signature on a plate in the breakarch. To compare this rich and warm style of dial with the Carney of about 30 years later is to note that the latter has quite different spandrels, of open Rococo form made up of interlocked 'C' scrolls with leaves and flowers, a comparatively narrow chapter ring without the internal

Engraved back plate of the movement of the clock by John Everell

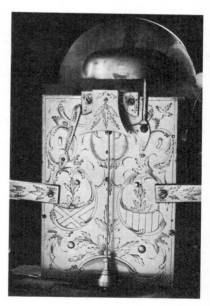

Engraved back plate of the movement of the clock by Peter Carney

Opposite page
Elaborate French astronomical clock in a veneered cabinet with gilded bronze mounts and patinated bronze sculptures; the subsidiary dials indicate mean and solar time, phases of the Moon and planetary motions; by Michael Stollewerck; about 1750. *Wallace Collection, London*

Above left
Cartel clock of English make but in the French Rococo style; carved and gilded wooden case; silvered dial with 'mock' pendulum; signed Marmaduke Storr, London; about 1755. *Lady Lever Art Gallery, Port Sunlight*

Above right
Design for a table clock in the Rococo taste by Thomas Johnson, London; Plate 16 from *150 New Designs* published in 1761; this plate dated 1756. *Victoria and Albert Museum, London*

marks for quarter hours, and most important of all a silvered centre dial with a seascape engraved upon it. In the scene a ship is attacking with gunfire a fortified tower, though curiously enough both the ship and the tower carry the same flag! But it is from the back plates of the movements of the Everell and Carney clocks that we see the absolute difference of their datable engraved designs. The Everell back plate is richly engraved with interweaving leafy scrolls, with flowers and a bird intermixed in the composition, with everything closely and tightly related, while the Carney clock back plate is at once seen to be lighter in style, making full use of counter-poised 'C' scrolls, again with leaves but with much 'chip' style cutting in short, repetitive strokes. Even the shapes of the pendulum cock plates are different, the Everell being rounded and heart-shaped in contrast to the Carney which is sharply defined with three concave edges. To recognise these differences is to see how the English bracket clock of the first half of the 18th century continued the use of shapes and motifs which owed their existence to the Baroque, while later clocks, up to about 1775 to 1780 were influenced by the lighter, more gay and more frivolous styles of French-derived Rococo. It should be added that both these clocks have verge escapements, but both pendulums are later replacements and not original to the clocks.

That fully mature French Rococo did at times penetrate the English scene, and was encouraged to do so by the cabinetmaking trade, may be shown by a clock signed by Marmaduke Storr of London, made about 1760, in a cartel case. Of carved and gilded wood this is similar in appearance to the French cartel clock we have seen, though being carved rather than cast it suggests that English brassfounders were not as confident and skilled in this sort of work as the French. Two designs for cartel clocks were published in *A New Book of Ornaments* in 1752 by Matthias Lock (a carver and furniture designer) assisted by H. Copland, both of whom were in Chippendale's employ, and a drawing for a clock by Thomas Johnson in 1756 shows what they would have liked but in fact rarely achieved as far as clocks were concerned. Johnson's design was from a series of prints published in 1758, without a title, but dedicated to the Right Honourable Lord Blakeney, which also included gerandoles, or wall-mounted candle sconces, of which many were actually made. Many gerandoles, unlike the Marmaduke Storr clock case, illustrated episodes from Aesop's Fables, and many too have Chinese figures and pagoda-shaped tops, in the chinoiserie style.

A final example in the present chapter is an English longcase clock with Rococo associations, being a magnificent specimen by the famous maker John Ellicott of London. John Ellicott (1706–72) of Swithin's Alley, Royal Exchange, was the son of an equally famous clockmaking father of the same Christian name. He is perhaps best remembered for his invention of the cylinder escapement in watches, and a particular style of temperature compensated pendulum for accurate regulator clocks. The clock here illustrated has a hollow pediment, making subtle use of the Rococo concave curve, but its particular and unusual feature is a group of contemporary prints pasted on the long trunk door and thinly varnished over. The prints are hand-coloured, copper plate engravings, each of the three depicting a gentleman offering a gift to a lady—a bird's nest, a flower and a fish. Entirely romantic and composed in rural settings, these prints were of a type most popular in the 1750s and 60s, taken or adapted from sources such as Antoine Watteau's paintings, or those of Nicolas Lancret, one of Watteau's imitators. Pictures such as François Boucher's 'Les Amours Pastorales' were issued as engraved prints and copied, for example, on tiles made by Sadler of Liverpool, frequently framed in Rococo scrolls. Only one other clock known to the author which has been treated in this way is an 'Act of Parliament' or tavern clock in the Bowes Museum near Durham, showing the influence of French art on clocks and furniture in the middle of the 18th century.

No account of the clocks of the 18th century in England or France would be complete without some reference to the astonishing scientific achievements of men such as John Harrison (1693–1776) in England, and Pierre le Roy (1717–85) in France. The importance of being able to calculate the longitude of a ship at sea by means of an accurate timekeeper from which the time at Greenwich could be compared with the 'local' time, wherever the vessel happened to be, has been told many times elsewhere, as has the long struggle of John Harrison in his efforts to reach that end. Harrison gave his life to the making of a machine which would satisfy the Board of Longitude, under the terms and conditions laid down by an Act of Parliament in 1714, and he succeeded in obtaining his reward when at a very advanced age. The prolonged and highly scientific endeavours undertaken by Harrison, with similar attempts by le Roy in France, produced a series of machines which, in their mechanical solution of complex problems and extraordinary quality of craftsmanship, might well be regarded as works of art, but an art which is different from what might be called the 'applied' or 'decorative' art of clock case design. Details of John Harrison's chronometers (as sea-going clocks are called) numbered 2 and 4 are illustrated here. Number 2 shows what might best be described as 'functional' art, rich

Longcase clock with musical work and quarter striking in a black japanned case; the trunk door is decorated with hand coloured engraved prints; signed John Ellicott, London; about 1755. *Lady Lever Art Gallery, Port Sunlight*

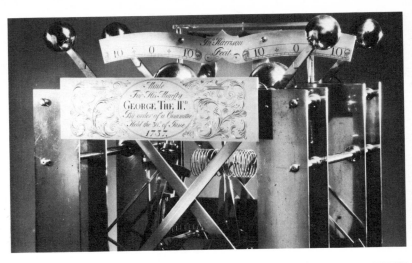

Engraved dedication plate from John Harrison's timekeeper No. 2, completed in 1739; this decorative treatment contrasts with the functional severity of the working parts. *National Maritime Museum, Greenwich*

Detail from the enamelled dial of John Harrison's timekeeper No. 4, completed in 1761; it illustrates the use of Rococo ornament on this superlative scientific instrument. *National Maritime Museum, Greenwich*

in the beauty of proportion, relationship of part to part, satisfying in the quality of wheelwork, balances, springs and anti-friction devices, designed to perform accurately at different temperatures and barometric pressures in the rolling and pitching cabin of a ship at sea. The functional idea of art as expressed by such machines should perhaps be called 'engineering art', and only a hundred years later, in the mid-19th century, men were beginning to see art in those terms, in terms where truth to purpose and truth to the right use of materials was the only way in which art could be conceived. In the early years of the present century the architect Tony Garnier wrote: 'Truth alone is beautiful. In architecture truth is the result of calculations made to satisfy known necessities with known materials'. How apt it would be to substitute, in the above quotation, the word 'horology' for 'architecture', and how good a description this would have been for Harrison's years of searching for truth in timekeeping.

The doctrine of functionalism is one mentioned later again, a doctrine which for us today has outmoded the historical styles of 'Gothic', 'Baroque', 'Rococo' and the like, but it is unlikely that Harrison himself saw matters in that way. When in 1737 he was completing his work on timekeeper No. 2, he had an experienced craftsman to letter the dedica-

Trade card of Thomas Gardner,
goldsmith and watchmaker, London;
about 1760

tion plate to King George II, engraved within a fine cartouche amidst flowing scrolls like the back plate of a domestic bracket clock. In No. 4, which is shaped like a much enlarged watch, just over 5 in (13 cm) in diameter, his dialmaker could not restrain himself from applying Rococo scrolls and flowers in four separate groupings outside the chapter ring. Such was the effect of 'fashion' on a machine of superlative engineering design. To watch the action of these superb machines in the Maritime Museum at Greenwich is to absorb an aesthetic experience quite unrelated to 'applied' design.

Fashion in clocks, as in almost everything else in our consumer society, is an important selling point, and it is appropriate that this chapter should close with the advertisement or trade card of Thomas Gardner (established by 1740–d 1770), a goldsmith and watchmaker who sold his goods and mended 'all sorts of Clocks and Watches' at his shop called the 'Dial' in the Minories near Aldgate, London. This trade card is a fragment of printed ephemera which has survived down the years, with its watches and watch dial, its silver tray and coffee pot, its tea kettle, hot water jug and castor, and its elaborate mantel clock in the French taste, festooning themselves around and within the swirling, scrolling designs of an extravagant cartouche of Rococo frivolity and conceit.

NEO-CLASSICISM
Elegance and Repose

To begin a chapter of a book on clocks with illustrations of two gravestones may seem strange, even though such memorials are important reminders of the passage of time. Their inclusion here is not to remind us of our mortality, but to show the difference in architectural and decorative styles which took place in England between the Rococo phase of the middle decades of the 18th century, and the Neo-Classical manner which supplanted it in the 1770s, or even slightly earlier.

The gravestone of John Marriott in the yard of Granby Church, Nottinghamshire, dated 1765, has its inscription within a decorative cartouche of carved 'C' and 'S' scrolls in exactly the same style as the Thomas Gardner trade card at the close of the fifth chapter—a full-blown Rococo design with a touch of 'Gothick' in the lettered inscription which was a part of Rococo we shall look at later. In complete contrast, the stone in memory of Elizabeth Bell from Long Clawson in the county of Leicestershire, dated 1792, with delicate symmetrical swags draped over and between oval-shaped flower heads known as paterae, and a central two-handled vase or urn at the top of the stone, is in the pure Neo-Classical style. While the former stone from Granby is restless, romantic and fussy, the latter design is cool, refined and classical, derived from a different source which in England is known as the Adam style.

To explain the origins in England of the Adam or Neo-Classical style of design the works of Robert Adam (1728–92), the 'father' of the style, Josiah Wedgwood (1730–95) and Matthew Boulton (1728–1809) will be mentioned in some detail because all three, in their own ways, were important participants in creating and popularising Neo-Classical ideas.

Robert Adam, who had early decided on an architectural career, made a prolonged tour of Italy starting in 1754, during which time he visited many famous Roman sites, notably the ruins of the Roman Palace of Diocletian at Spalato, now known as Split, on the Adriatic coast of Yugoslavia. In the company of his brother James he also visited the partially excavated remains of the Roman cities of Pompeii and Herculaneum. Both these towns had been completely devastated by the eruption of the volcano Vesuvius on 24 August, AD 79, and the archaeological investigation of these sites began in earnest during the 18th century, at Pompeii in 1748 (although the first remains were located as early as 1594), and at Herculaneum in 1738. The preservation, almost intact, of Roman houses, furniture, schemes of decoration, wall paintings, mosaics, sculptures and many other artefacts attracted numerous men of letters and culture from all parts of Europe, perhaps the most influential being Johann Joachim Winckelmann (1717–68), the first great German art historian who, through his writings, has been called one of the founders of the Neo-Classical style. Here, at Pompeii and Herculaneum, the Adam brothers were to see, as had never been seen before, intimate interiors of original Roman decoration of the first century AD, which must have been enormously stimulating and exciting to architects who had been nurtured on Palladian standards, based on the monumental architecture of the noble ruins of Imperial Rome. In Rome also, in the 1750s, Adam came under the influence of that great Venetian architect and designer Giovanni Battista Piranesi (1720–78), whose imaginative and archaeologically inspired romantic designs in his *Carceri d'Invenzione*, and his topographical etchings of ancient and modern Rome in *Vedute di Roma* (first issued in 1745), had a considerable effect in spreading the 'antique' Roman taste in England. Robert Adam returned to England in 1758 with a new vocabulary of architectural and decorative motifs—the vase, urn, delicate filigree mouldings, fluted arcading, ovals, diamonds, rectangles, winged sphinxes, dolphins, griffins, draped festoons, rams' head masks, acanthus, honeysuckle, pendant catkins and husking. He saw these features as part of a new and lighter, more graceful style, as part of a more intimate approach to interior design, in contrast to the heavy and somewhat ponderous style of Palladian interiors, or the fussy and restless fashion for Rococo. His taste in colour was influenced, too, using pastel tones of pink, pale green, soft blues, lilac and white, with limited use of gold, in contrast again to Palladian and Baroque. Numerous country houses were re-planned and altered by Adam on his return from Italy, such as Harewood House in Yorkshire, Shardeloes in Buckinghamshire, Syon House in Middlesex, Newby Hall in Yorkshire, and many others. As an interior decorator, Robert Adam made himself responsible for the complete designs for interiors, for carpets which reflected the patterns of ceilings, for lock plates and other door furniture, even for such details as fire-irons and fenders, and of course for the furniture. It is in the context of the fashionable re-designing of such interiors that clocks of Neo-Classical taste should be considered, interiors by Adam and his many imitators.

Below left
Gravestone in the churchyard at Granby, Nottinghamshire, illustrating Rococo decoration and lettering; dated 1765

Below right
Gravestone in the churchyard at Long Clawson, Leicestershire, illustrating Neo-Classical ornament and lettering; dated 1792

A drawing from the 1773 edition of *The Works in Architecture of Robert and James Adam Esquires* shows a pier glass and side table with a design for a clock in which the elements of the separate items are subtly linked together to form a satisfying whole, in which the clock is a part and not an independent item. Winged griffins, draped female figures and tazzas are repeated in the looking glass mounts, the double-branched candelabra and the clock itself, while honeysuckle springing above the mirror is echoed by similar sprays beneath the pier table edge, encircled with festooned husking. There is much here to connect French taste with Adam's designs, for this is the expression of a courtly style, but unfortunately few such furnishing schemes involving clocks have survived today, in their original settings.

A magnificent clock in the Neo-Classical taste, at the Lady Lever Art Gallery in Port Sunlight, is superlative by any standards, for the quality of its movement and that of its case. The clock bears the name 'Vulliamy LONDON' on the bottom left front edge, and it was made about 1790. Its maker, Benjamin Vulliamy (1747–1811) was the son of a Swiss clockmaker Justin Vulliamy (1712–97) who had set up his business in London about 1730. A portrait of Benjamin survives in which there also appears a clock not unlike the Lady Lever Gallery example, both clocks—the real and the depicted—being dominated by a draped classical figure of a lady leaning over a globe in the painted clock, and an urn in the Port Sunlight example. The figure is of Calliope, one of the nine mythological Muses, who presided over music and heroic poetry and was said to be the mother of Orpheus by Apollo. She is made of Derby biscuit (unglazed) porcelain, purchased from William Duesbury, the proprietor of the famous Derby porcelain factory, where many exquisite porcelain figures in this material were made. One might say that this figure of Calliope, sometimes draping herself over an urn or vase, sometimes posed with an anchor symbolic of Hope, and frequently found in the decorative art of the late 18th century, might almost be described as an archetypal form symbolising the Neo-Classical style. In the Port Sunlight clock the shoulder of the vase is the clock dial itself, rotating horizontally, the time on the hour and minute bands indicated by the forked tongue of a serpent, the movement of the clock being housed in the plinth below. On the clock in the portrait of Vulliamy the plinth carries the dial, while above is a globe of the Earth, rotating in 24 hours, over which Calliope is poised and assisted in her contemplation by a cupid or cherub.

The plinth of the Port Sunlight Vulliamy clock is mounted with an oval plaque or medallion on which a figure of Apollo with his lyre in white relief is modelled. The medallion is made of a hard type of vitreous unglazed stoneware or semi-porcelain, known by the name of jasperware, and it was provided by that industrial, scientific and artistic genius of the 18th century, Josiah Wedgwood. More, perhaps, than any other single manufacturer, Josiah Wedgwood popularised and promoted the Neo-Classicism of Robert Adam in the 18th century through his basalt and jasperware pottery, and the style still remains popular today through the small decorative objects with white relief figures on a blue ground, made by the present Wedgwood company. Josiah first introduced his jasperware in 1774 (so named because of its resemblance to an opaque type of natural quartz known as jasper) after years of experimentation. Most of the subject matter in the jasperware medallions and other objects is based on classical prototypes of the same style as those employed by Adam. In partnership with Thomas Bentley

Mantel clock with figure in Derby porcelain; gilded bronze case and mounts; Wedgwood medallion in jasperware; marble base; signed Vulliamy, London; about 1790. *Lady Lever Art Gallery, Port Sunlight*

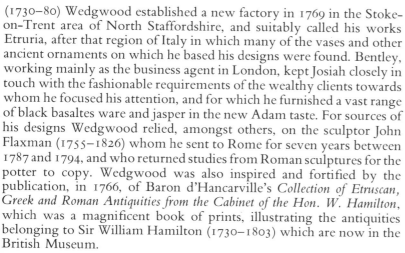

Portrait in oils of Benjamin Vulliamy; artist unknown. *Clockmakers' Company Museum, London*

(1730–80) Wedgwood established a new factory in 1769 in the Stoke-on-Trent area of North Staffordshire, and suitably called his works Etruria, after that region of Italy in which many of the vases and other ancient ornaments on which he based his designs were found. Bentley, working mainly as the business agent in London, kept Josiah closely in touch with the fashionable requirements of the wealthy clients towards whom he focused his attention, and for which he furnished a vast range of black basaltes ware and jasper in the new Adam taste. For sources of his designs Wedgwood relied, amongst others, on the sculptor John Flaxman (1755–1826) whom he sent to Rome for seven years between 1787 and 1794, and who returned studies from Roman sculptures for the potter to copy. Wedgwood was also inspired and fortified by the publication, in 1766, of Baron d'Hancarville's *Collection of Etruscan, Greek and Roman Antiquities from the Cabinet of the Hon. W. Hamilton*, which was a magnificent book of prints, illustrating the antiquities belonging to Sir William Hamilton (1730–1803) which are now in the British Museum.

Other clocks with medallions from Wedgwood's Etruria works are known, of which two are cited here, the medallions being set in marble cases. The first is a mantelpiece clock at 20 St James's Square in London, a superb marble clock with triple urns above linked with arabesque scrolls, Vitruvian scrolls on the front of the base and a pair of circular Wedgwood blue and white jasper plaques in the centres of the supporting columns (see p. 101). Miss Alison Kelly, an eminent Wedgwood historian, has pointed out that the figures on the left were designed by Flaxman, emblematic of Mercury joining the hands of France and England to commemorate the commercial Treaty of 1786, and a figure of 'Liberty' beneath a classical arch on the right. Medallions such as these were not just for the ornamentation of clocks, but had many uses in furniture, fireplaces, jewellery or simply as decorative framed plaques.

The second clock with a Wedgwood medallion is a marble timepiece by Benjamin Vulliamy in the British Museum, the motif this time being simply of three Bacchanalian cupids designed, it is said, by Lady Diana Beauclerk. The increasingly popular imperial eagle above the clock which will later be seen to have influenced the design of clocks in America, and the black patinated bronze sphinxes, are typical of these much used figures at the time.

The Wedgwood/Vulliamy clocks mentioned above are all, excluding the clock movement itself, the corporate efforts of different craftsmen in different materials, coming together to produce a fine, unified work, aimed to attract a discerning customer of educated taste. Of the supplier of the carved marble elements we as yet know nothing, but the gilded bronzes were almost certainly from the foundry of another industrialist of genius and foresight, Matthew Boulton, silversmith and brassfounder of Birmingham. Matthew Boulton came into the metalworking business through his father's involvement in the button-making, or 'toy trade' industry as it was then known. He started life in a comparatively small way, but succeeded to such an extent that by 1759 he began to build a large new manufactury for silverware and other metal goods at Handsworth Heath, between Wolverhampton and Birmingham, which he called the Soho Manufactory, advertising it with prints in French as well as English, for European trade was his firm intention. Almost as Wedgwood had enlisted the support of Thomas Bentley, so Boulton encouraged an informal partnership with John Fothergill about 1762, a man of cosmopolitan accomplishments who forwarded Boulton's business at the London end. Wedgwood and Boulton belonged to that intimate circle of distinguished men of letters, science and industry which regularly met together under the title of *The Lunar Society of Birmingham* from 1766. That such an organisation existed is evidence enough of the growing importance of industrial and scientific enterprise in the provincial centres of the English north and midlands.

A design of clock which is firmly linked to Matthew Boulton is one known as the 'Titus' clock (see p. 101). The idea for the design was first conceived in 1771 and several were made in the following years, presumably to meet orders by customers who had seen the model in the Boulton and Fothergill pattern book. In the same general composition of a standing figure by a plinth as in the Calliope clock, the Roman Emperor Titus stands beside an urn on a plinth, his gilded bronze or 'ormolu' figure in oratorial pose. The base, plinth and urn of this case are of marble and the cover of the urn, or vase, has a 'flame' or torchère finial and pierced surface, made in this way to allow the fumes from burning perfume to escape, for this is a cassolette. A Roman guilloche

design surrounds the shoulder of the vase and festoons of husking hang from applied mask heads. A gilded plaque on the front of the vase is engraved *diem perdidi*, relating to a statement Titus is recorded as having made, that he had 'lost a day' because he had passed a day during which he had done no act of generosity. The movement in the Titus clock is French, by a maker of the name of Caillard, imported from Paris to fit the case. The white enamel dial and the 'beetle and poker' hands are purely English in style, closely resembling those to be seen on pocket watches of the time.

Many other clock cases are known for which Boulton produced parts, but one further clock in the royal collections, originally made for King George III in 1771 deserves special mention, for it was designed by a famous architect, Sir William Chambers (1723–96). Chambers is probably best known today for his original design for Somerset House in London, and familiar to many through the splendid Chinese pagoda in Kew Gardens, designed in 1760 and a famous example of chinoiserie in English garden ornament. His clock case for George III is in Neo-Classical taste, though somewhat heavier in style than it would have been, had it been designed by Adam. Rams' heads, placed like those on the Lady Lever Art Gallery Vulliamy clock, adorn each corner of the square case, with festoons and swags below and a laurel wreath beneath the dial. The top is adorned with a tazza, with handled ewers as finials at the corners. The superb quality of the metalwork on this case is set off to perfection against the front and side panels of polished blue-john stone which was a favourite material in the hands of Boulton, of richer colour and deeper hue than either porcelain, marble or alabaster. Blue-john is a form of fluorspar which was mined near Castleton in Derbyshire, and

Above left
Mantel clock with marble base, patinated bronze sphinxes, gilded eagle above, Wedgwood jasperware medallion; signed Benjamin Vulliamy, London; about 1790. *British Museum, London*

Above right
Mantel clock in gilded bronze with polished blue-john stone panels; movement by Thomas Wright, the King's clockmaker, later altered by B. L. Vulliamy; case designed by Sir William Chambers and made by Matthew Boulton; 1771. *By gracious permission of H.M. The Queen, Royal Collection, Windsor Castle*

Right
Drawing of the pediment for a door case
from *A Complete Body of Architecture*
by Isaac Ware, published 1756

Below
Longcase clock in mahogany with
Rococo, Gothick and Neo-Classical
detailing; silvered, gilded and painted
dial; signed William Kirk, Stockport;
about 1770. *Lady Lever Art Gallery, Port
Sunlight*

Boulton used this as the base for many of his decorative vases, just as
Wedgwood used variegated and marbled clay for the bodies of his
ornamental pieces. The clock movement itself was made by one
Thomas Wright, official watchmaker to the king, and was of month
duration, with a plain white enamel dial and wavy, blued-steel hands of
exactly the design as are found on many bracket clocks of the period,
such as the Peter Carney in the fifth chapter. Apparently the movement
was later altered by Benjamin Louis Vulliamy (1780–1854), the son of
the Benjamin we have already met, and the clock stands today in the
Queen's private rooms at Windsor Castle, flanked by a pair of Boulton's perfume-burner vases. In spite of this clock being a royal commission, designed by the king's own architect, Matthew Boulton saw no
reason why he should not make another similar clock which he offered
for public sale in the following year, but that is another story.

In case it should be thought that all late 18th-century clocks in
England followed the refined quality of Neo-Classical design, it is
important to understand that the making of conventional brass-dial
clocks in timber cases, both bracket and longcase, went on as before, for
those that have been discussed represent the latest designs for the
highest in the land, much inspired by Continental practice. As far as
ordinary clocks are concerned, the classical proportions of Palladian
Georgian continued to hold sway, influenced by Rococo details, especially in the dial spandrel mounts and occasionally in the casework.
Thomas Chippendale's excursions into 'Gothick' in the 1750s and 60s
had its effect in case design, and the swan's neck pediment became a
more or less standard feature, especially in clocks from the north of
England. The swan's neck pediment is a form of 'broken pediment'
which came into vogue early in the 18th century in both architecture
and furniture, and was not unknown in the 17th century. A good
example is a design for a door case published by Isaac Ware in 1756 in *A
Complete Body of Architecture*. The swan's neck form consists of two 'S'
shaped scrolls, symmetrically arranged and terminating internally with
carved and gilded floral bosses. Although the motif is not Rococo in
origin it was taken up in the middle of the century and it is seen on
bookcases and cabinets in Chippendale's 1754 *Director*.

An example of the mixed use of Rococo and Neo-Classical motifs in a north country clock of about 1770 is one by William Kirk of Stockport, then a small town near Manchester. Its tall mahogany case is crowned with a swan's neck pediment above a break-arch dial, the space between these features, the tympanum, being filled with a pierced fret, richly scrolled. The fluted, free-standing columns of the hood have gilded Corinthian capitals and bases, but the most significant part of the case is the trunk and the long trunk door. The top of the door is shaped in three pointed arches, the central arch of o-gee form, terminating in a finial, while the corner columns of the trunk are not classical but are of triple-coupled shafts derived directly from Gothic architecture, as is the top of the door. The Gothic motifs revived in the 18th century are usually referred to as 'Gothick', a mannerism much encouraged by the antiquarian activities of Horace Walpole (1717–97), who published his mediaeval-style 'terror' novel *The Castle of Otranto* in 1765, and converted his house at Strawberry Hill, Twickenham, into a Gothick mansion. Thomas Chippendale took up the style and many pieces of furniture in his published designs contain elements of Gothick, associated with Rococo scrolls and other fanciful imagery. A 'blind fret' design at the top of the trunk of the Kirk clock reminds one of Chippendale's Chinese frets, but curiously associated with Rococo and Gothick, on this splendid case, is relief carved ornament down the centre of the door. This feature is Neo-Classical in style, with a large two-handled urn at its centre, and the inlaid patterns on the trunk offsets and plinth are also Neo-Classic, arranged like pendant husking, but of Gothic o-gee curves. The whole case illustrates a most curious mixture of influences—Gothick, Rococo, Neo-Classical and Palladian—which northern clocks, two hundred miles from the London centre of fashion, tend to display. Here is a latent stylistic conservatism, touched, but not transformed by the dictates of fashionable taste, and entirely symbolic of the aspirations of the rising manufacturing class. The dial of the Kirk clock is something of a mixture of motifs too, for the engraved and gilded centre expresses Neo-Classical rather than Rococo forms, and the silvered chapter ring is fitted to a painted plate, heralding a change in the style of longcase dials which were almost all painted by the early 19th century.

The northern counties of England, especially Lancashire and Yorkshire, produced some outstanding clockmakers in the late 18th century, and a 'school' of clockmaking developed which had little to do with the London fashions, but rather belonged to the rising wealth and prosperity of the industrial birthplace of the nation. One such maker was William Barker (*d* 1787) of Wigan, most famous for a great astronomical clock which he built in the late 1770s. A more humble clock from his shop is illustrated, signed *Wigan* on the back plate and *Warrington* on the dial. The reason for this idiosyncrasy has never been resolved, though it might simply have been a mistake on the part of the dial painter. It is a charming clock, decorated throughout in the Neo-Classical way, with an oval cartouche, a pair of matching paterae like those on Elizabeth Bell's gravestone, draped husking from bow-tied ribbons and a flower on the pendulum cock. All is engraved on the back plate, while the case too has decoration in the same style, painted on its ebonised surface. The overall form is the same as the Peter Carney bracket clock but its painted dial with concentric calendar hand, its 'rolling' moon and its painted spandrels with rustic scenes symbolising the seasons of the year, projects the fashion for painted, cheaper dials which were to follow, especially in the 19th century longcase clock.

Before leaving the English style of the late 18th century to see what

Bracket clock of ebonised wood with painted Neo-Classical decoration; the dial is painted and has a rolling Moon and date ring inside the chapters; signed William Barker, Warrington on the dial and Wigan on the back plate; about 1770. *Merseyside County Museums, Liverpool*

was happening in France, two final clocks must be shown. One, by
Thomas Lister (1748–1814) of Halifax, has a superb mahogany case
with Adam-style ornament down the trunk door and plinth, yet with
Gothick corner columns like the William Kirk of Stockport. The other
is a magnificent and monumental instrument in a mahogany case of
majestic classical proportions, with a barometer set in the door and a
dial of considerable complexity. A sweep-seconds hand and calendar
hand, together with those for the hours and minutes, stand out against a
diamond fretted centre, inside the chapter ring. This style of diapered
engraving is peculiar to northern Lancashire clocks and owes its origin
to Chinese Rococo. Subsidiary dials indicate the tunes played on its set
of bells every four hours, with a tune for each day of the week,
automatically advanced, and the phases of the Moon and high tides at
Liverpool. The crowning glory of the clock is the upper dial with its
gilded Sun which rotates once each day, and against slowly moving
shutters shows the time of its rising and setting for each day of the year.
This astronomical musical clock was made by Joseph Finney
(c 1708–72) of Liverpool in the last decade of his life, and unlike most
provincial makers Finney had business dealings in clocks and scientific
instruments with King George III.

It is strange that, although we now know a great deal about Joseph
Finney and the clocks and instruments for which he was responsible, we
know nothing whatever about the maker of the fabulous case in which
his astronomical clock was housed. That anonymity should be normal
for humble and common articles of furniture is understandable, but for
a magnificent piece of cabinetwork such as this not to be identifiable
seems unfair to its long-gone maker. Many fine cabinetmakers worked
in the growing industrial towns of Liverpool, Leeds, Manchester,
Sheffield and several other places in the Midlands and northern areas.
Cabinetwork of equal quality may still be seen in domestic furnishings
for the houses of wealthy merchants, in church altars and pulpits, for
board rooms and banking houses. It must be remembered that a clock
case, however fine, was but another domestic furnishing item—of
quality indeed but no more meriting special identification than the
equally fine cabinetwork and joinery which went into the building of

thousands of Georgian houses. Clock cases were commissioned by the clockmaker, not as works of art in themselves, but merely as useful and sufficiently imposing structures to house the clock movements and dials, for it was the dial of the clock which carried the maker's or retailer's name. Occasionally, one comes across the label of a specialist clock casemaker pasted inside (see also the following chapter), and one is shown here of a man who was plying his trade for the London clockmakers, illustrating how even a humble trade label could be ornamented with the tazza and husked festoons of the Adam style.

The relationship of the importance of a case relative to the clock which is housed inside it is completely reversed when the subject of French clocks of the 18th century is raised. Many French clock cases were named by the ébénistes and bronze founders, or by the sculptors of the ornaments and figures, indicating that the cases were important either as works of art or furnishing accessories, to which the clock was a necessary though not superior adjunct.

French clocks of the third and last quarters of the 18th century are normally described as Louis XVI, after the famous king who succeeded to the throne in 1774, was arrested shortly after the Revolution in 1791 and finally guillotined in 1793. The effect on clockmaking of the French Revolution and the troubled years between 1789 and 1799 was disastrous in that the French aristocracy, on whose patronage the clockmakers had thrived, were in many cases hounded from their châteaux which, with the royal palaces and other symbols of hereditary privilege, were either destroyed or became the property of the state and people. Some famous clockmakers, such as Abraham-Louis Breguet (1747–1823), of Swiss nationality but working in Paris, were forced to flee the capital. In his case it was partly because of his nationality but mostly because of his contact with, and sympathy for, the Court and its aristocratic members.

By the second half of the 18th century virtually all French clockmakers with any pretensions to excellence had set up their workshops in Paris, though by this time French clockmakers were 'buying in' their rough movements from specialist makers in the provinces. The range of styles and designs of cases which were produced and which are loosely called Louis XVI is so vast that no attempt can be made to itemise them all; but unlike the earlier periods there were only two basic types, the mantel clock and the precision clock (which was either mantel or longcase), though the mantel clocks were of incredible variety and form.

French Louis XVI mantel clocks of the best quality scarcely ever used wood in their construction, nor were they usually entirely of cast bronze. Louis XVI is a period which saw the increasing use of marble, alabaster, porcelain and enamelled copper in association with gilded bronze castings and mounts. Epitomising the fanciful nature of the style, and in its way also being related to the developing scientific ideas of the time, is a clock in the form of a balloon, conceived within the overall manner of the Neo-Classical idiom. In gilded bronze and white marble the clock itself is within a case shaped like a balloon, of the hydrogen-filled type and not a hot-air balloon. From a fine wire net above the 'balloon' a basket is suspended on chains, the whole creation being elegantly supported by symmetrical female-headed and acanthus modelled scrolling brackets, rising from an oval marble base on turned bronze feet, with the pendulum bob appearing as a miniature balloon behind. This superlative creation is by Adam L'Échopié, a first-rate maker of the time, and the type of clock is often known as a Montgolfière. The brothers Joseph and Étienne Montgolfier were the first to make possible a human ascent in a hot-air balloon, after experimenting

Monumental longcase clock in mahogany, with double pairs of Corinthian columns, Ionic trunk columns, break-arch dial with swan's neck pediment and base with quoins; the movement indicates the time of the rising and setting of the Sun and plays tunes every four hours; barometer in the door; signed Joseph Finney, Liverpool; about 1770. *Merseyside County Museums, Liverpool*

Above left
French mantel clock in the form of a balloon; gilded bronze and white marble; commemorating the interest in ballooning towards the end of the 18th century; signed L'Échopié à Paris; about 1785

Above right
French mantel clock in the form of the base of a fluted pillar; Sèvres porcelain on a marble base with gilded mounts; signed Dubois à Paris; about 1780.
Wallace Collection, London

with animals as astronauts, on 21 November 1783. However, the balloon ascent probably commemorated by the L'Échopié clock was that of the first hydrogen-filled balloon which took off from the Jardin des Tuileries on 1 December 1783 and landed at Nesle, 27 miles away. The clock should not, therefore, be called a Montgolfière, but perhaps rather a 'Charles' after the name of the professor who was the first to build a successful gas balloon.

Mantel clocks in the form of a fluted column remind one of the interest in classical ruins which so strongly influenced the decorative arts of the late 18th century. They especially remind one of the Roman and other Italian ruins depicted in the etchings of Giovanni Battista Piranesi (1720–78) whose published works had an enormous influence on European architects and landscape gardeners, or the paintings of Gavin Hamilton (1723–98) in the Rotunda at Kedleston. The clock by Germaine Dubois might reasonably be called a pillar clock, for it consists of a columnar plinth surmounted by a covered tazza in glazed white Sèvres porcelain, with underglaze blue and gold, hung about with a gilded garland of leaves and flowers.

A form of French clock which does not appear to have any English parallel is the lyre clock in which the movement is supported on an oval conical base by means of a frame in the form of a Greek lyre, an instrument often depicted in the hands of Apollo in classical reliefs. A 'sun-burst' head at the top is the suspension point for a pendulum, the

French mantel clock, known as a lyre clock; case in royal blue Sèvres porcelain with gilded bronze mounts; the pendulum bob consists of a ring of cut quartz stones round the dial; signed Kinable à Paris; about 1780. *Victoria and Albert Museum, London*

Mantel clock in biscuit porcelain, modelled with a youth and maiden—possibly Venus and Adonis—with cupid above; movement signed Gavelle l'aîné à Paris; about 1780. Originally this case would have had a glass shade. *The Bowes Museum, Barnard Castle, Co. Durham*

bob of which is a ring of brilliant–cut quartz crystal stones which frames the dial and swings gently from side to side, sparkling and reflecting candlelight in a most attractive way. The mechanical arrangement of a pendulum suspended above rather than below the movement was no particular problem, and the example shown is made of royal blue Sèvres porcelain with gilded mounts. The dial has four concentric hands, for the normal hours and minutes, for the date on the inner chapter ring edge, and a hand for the month which is indicated on the outside edge, each month having its Zodiacal sign enamelled in a semi-circular reserve. The lyre as a basic form for these clocks is a pointer to the revival of interest in Greek, rather than Roman antiquity, which was to become more strongly felt by the end of the 18th century, and the shape was an influence in the design of early American domestic clocks.

Of the countless extraordinary and imaginative designs which were made by outstanding French craftsmen in the later 18th century, it is surely those which contain human figures that capture the eye most effectively, and which astonish the senses in their quality of modelling and composition. Small figure bronzes were popular in France from the days in the 16th century when Benvenuto Cellini worked there; yet later Neo-Classical female semi-nudes with flowing drapery often seem cold and lifeless, without the warmth and voluptuousness of earlier figures of the Rococo style. The figures on a clock by Gavelle l'aîné of about 1780, made entirely in unglazed porcelain, are of much greater technical complexity than the single figure of Derby biscuit porcelain on the English clock by Vulliamy. A youth and a maiden, probably Venus and Adonis, disport with a cherub or cupid above, and it is fairly clear that the cupid will soon be captured and crowned with floral bouquets which await him, above the dial and in the left hand of the lady delivered from a basket, not seen at the back. The metal movement is held in this porcelain clock by means of two long screws and straps which link the dial and bezel at the front to a plate or ring at the rear, a system which became universal for fitting standard French movements into cases of many styles and materials throughout the century which was to follow.

A final type of French clock must conclude this review, for the full richness of the clocks of Louis XVI type would take a complete volume to describe. In scientific terms the finest French clocks of the late 18th century were the régulateur and its smaller companion the petit régulateur à demi-seconde, that is a small mantel precision clock with its pendulum oscillating in half seconds. In both these types of clock the common feature is a large and heavy grid-iron pendulum, of great importance to the accurate timekeeping of the clock because these maintain the same length (and therefore the same rate of vibration) in varying temperatures. Heavy grid-iron pendulums with large flat bobs are strong visual elements in the appeal of these clocks, conveying to the casual observer a strong sense of scientific accuracy as well as being so in fact. Intentionally left fully visible, they are the first domestic type of clock we have seen since the Middle Ages in which the mechanism has become part of the visual appeal, a shift in emphasis which led in due course to the skeleton clock of the 19th century.

In spite of the extremes of decorative treatment in the architectural and sculptural cases of French clocks of the time of Louis XVI, it was a period when a small group of French horologists of immense skill were at work producing masterpieces of the clockmaker's art. Even Louis XVI himself, like his neighbour King George III across the English Channel, was interested in clockwork mechanisms and is known to have investigated their workings. Of this small group of great clockmakers, including names such as Robert Robin (1742–99), Jean-André Le Paute (1720–89) and Antide Janvier (1751–1835), one of the most famous was Ferdinand Berthoud (1727–1807) whose reputation, with that of Pierre Le Roy (1717–85) was as high in the history of horology as Harrison, Arnold, Earnshaw or Mudge in England.

The longcase régulateur, of which few examples remain compared with the vast number of mantel clocks, is perhaps the ultimate triumph

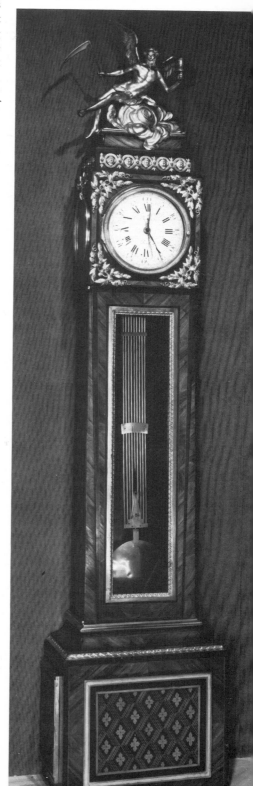

French régulateur veneered in kingwood and tulipwood with gilded bronze mounts; dial in enamelled copper; the grid-iron pendulum is a strong visual element in the design; movement signed Robin à Paris; case by Balthazar Lieutaud; about 1770. *Victoria and Albert Museum, London*

French mantel clock in a gilded bronze case set with enamelled porcelain panels; signed Cronier à Paris; about 1785. *Wallace Collection, London*

of French clockmaking, and at its best a superb creation both technically and in terms of its case. As a scientific instrument, English regulators were housed in comparatively simple cases, their primary purpose being to hold firmly the accurate movement. They were mostly used either for astronomical observatories or on the premises of a working clockmaker, and not as domestic clocks in the ordinary sense. French régulateurs, however, as well as being of consummate quality as clocks, were also housed in cases of the latest style and elegance of finish. The one shown here is by Robert Robin in a case designed by Balthazar Lieutaud who worked in Paris from 1772 to 1807. The tall rectangular case, of distinguished proportions and attractively veneered in king-wood and tulipwood, both of which came from Brazil, is embellished only at the top with floral mounts in gilded bronze to draw attention to its plain white enamelled dial; and the crowning glory is a figure of

Time raised high aloft with his scythe and hour-glass. This is a clock of great dignity which must have looked magnificent in its original French interior.

It is useful to compare Robin's 'scientific' instrument and the treatment of its case with a porcelain panelled rectangular mantel clock by Jean-Baptiste-François Cronier, which would be displayed on the chimneypiece of the 'salon', while Robin's régulateur is clearly for the library or study. The Cronier clock is panelled on the front and sides with plaques of Sèvres porcelain, done in underglaze blue and on-glaze gold, but the reserve below the dial of a charming basket of flowers, enamelled and fired to the porcelain base, is a typical feature of late 18th-century decorative art, with its purple bow of ribbons at the top.

Rarely today is it possible to find original documents which record the purchase and delivery of a clock almost two centuries ago; but through the kindness of Mr David Barker, who found the papers, we can bring the 18th century to a close with a quotation from a bill and letter relating to the delivery of a longcase clock to an English house in 1794. The clock was bought by Godfrey Wentworth Esquire, of Woolley Hall near Wakefield, Yorkshire, from John Holmes, clockmaker, of The Strand, London. The bill reads:

London May 10th 1794

Godfrey Wentworth Esqr
Bought of John Holmes 156 Strand

A new eight day Clock name Holmes London in a Mahogany Case with a wooden gilt pendulum & to keep going while winding up	£ 10	s 10	
A long packing Case, packing & porterage to the Inn		14	6
	£11	4	6

and the letter with it:

Sir

The Rev^d^ Mr Raine having done my Father the favor to order a Clock for you, I beg leave to acquaint you that it was delivered on the 10th Ins^t^ at the Blossoms Inn in Lawrence Lane, to be forwarded by the Waggon, and left at the White Hart Inn, in Wakefield. I hope it will arrive safe and please: I have taken the liberty of sending the account of it above, and on the opposite beg leave to trouble you with directions that it may be properly fixed up

I have the honor to be Sir
Your most obedient & most Hble Servant
Wm Holmes
N° 156 Strand London
May 13th 1794

The clock was one of good quality, with maintaining power to keep it going while winding, and with a wooden pendulum rod which was the best material for a pendulum not compensated for temperature variation. The instructions for fitting it up referred to in the letter are almost identical to those quoted at the end of the third chapter, some hundred and twenty years earlier, in which it would appear that all the parts were fitted in place in the clock case, screwed down with pieces of wood to avoid disturbance and ready to go when the packing was withdrawn. Short of employing the services of a local clockmaker to assist in the setting up, this was the only way that a London maker could more or less guarantee that the clock would be set going properly. For anyone who has ever had trouble with the gut lines on an English longcase clock, it would be interesting to know whether Mr Holmes delivered the clock unwound or wound.

EMPIRE AND REGENCY
Expanding Horizons

American tall clock; the English painted dial has the initials of the clockmaker Benjamin Clark Gilman of Exeter, New Hampshire; about 1800. *New Hampshire Historical Society*

The story of clock case design followed so far has been entirely concerned with European types apart from a brief excursion to Japan. As the cradle of western civilisation and scientific development Europe led the world, but by the end of the 18th century the growing community in North America had not only established its roots, but had declared its own independence in 1776, after a costly war against the army of George III. By 1783 England had recognised the independence of the 13 original colonies, and in 1789 a new constitution had been drawn up and George Washington, the first President of the new republic, was chosen. This new country, made up of the immigrant populations of western European countries, was to grow into a vital, pioneering and powerful nation, and its contribution to clockmaking was to be vital too, ultimately breaking down the cherished conservatism of the European manufactures in a dramatic and significant way.

Since the original colonists of North America had come from Europe—many from England—it is natural that the clocks they first made should have been designed on traditional lines, and the longcase clock appeared early on the American scene, known by Americans as a tall case clock. During the colonial period many clocks were imported complete from Europe, but as time went on only those parts of clocks which were difficult and costly to make in a virgin country were imported, such as movements and dials, while cases were made of native timber, but still more or less in English style. By the end of the 18th century large numbers of tall case clocks were being produced, and today it is sometimes difficult to tell whether or not the movement and dial was English or American, especially the movement which might have been assembled in America from English parts or partly finished castings. Dials are usually easier to judge, and many English dials are to be found on early American tall case clocks. An example is illustrated here by Benjamin Clark Gilman (1763–1835) of Exeter, New Hampshire, of about 1800. Gilman was a silversmith, engraver, builder, engineer, clockmaker and instrument maker, typifying the entrepreneurial spirit of early American tradesmen. Its locally made case, in maple, birch and pine, is a standard style of English longcase, but its cresting of pierced scrolls is typical of a wide range of American variations which adorn the tops of hoods of tall clocks. The brass and steel movement is also locally made, economising in brass by using 'cut away' plates which were common in New Hampshire, but the painted dial was imported from Birmingham, the name WILSON : BIRMN appearing on the dial false-plate. James Wilson of Charles Street, Birmingham, was one of the many specialist dialmakers and painters in that town at the end of the 18th and beginning of the 19th century, and Benjamin Clark Gilman was content to inscribe his initials B.C.G. on the visible part of the dial.

It is only possible to touch briefly on the vast number of magnificent, if somewhat 'primitive', types of tall case clocks which survive in the United States, but a maker about whom much is known is Daniel

Burnap (1759–1838) of East Windsor, Connecticut. The shop records of Burnap give a remarkably clear idea of his manner of working, while his links with the English tradition are underlined through his apprenticeship, at about 15 years of age, to the English-born clockmaker Thomas Harland (1735–1807) who had settled in Norwich, Connecticut, in 1773. Somewhat like Gilman of New Hampshire, Burnap did not work exclusively on clocks, for to quote his own advertisement of 1791, he 'takes this method to inform the publick that although he works in many other branches common to those in the silversmith line, as also Surveyor's Compasses, Watch repairing, &c, yet notwithstanding Clock Making is intended as the governing business of his shop, and is determined that no pains shall be wanting to merit the approbation of his customers. Clocks of various kinds may be had at his shop in East Windsor, on short notice on the most reasonable terms (warranted).'

From Daniel Burnap's account books it is notable that he made many clocks for sale without cases, for the cases could be made by cabinet-makers whenever and wherever they were required. The separation of clockmaker and casemaker is clear from Burnap's accounts and although the names of some of the casemakers he employed are known, it has not been possible to identify any Burnap clock case to a particular maker. In 1795 Burnap advertised for 'A journeyman Cabinet-Maker, who is a workman at Clock-Case making, may meet with employment by applying to Daniel Burnap, of East Windsor, who wishes to contract for the making of 15 or 20 cases.' Penrose R. Hoopes, Burnap's biographer, records that because of this advertisement one Joseph Bartlet was employed to make cases at £1.10.00 each, and that in 18 weeks he completed 22 cases from lumber and hardware, earning £33.00.00 in wages. Daniel Burnap's own musical clock with six tunes indicated on the dial, now at the Wadsworth Atheneum in Hartford, is in a case of extreme simplicity, closely modelled on the contemporary provincial English style, with trunk corner columns and swan's neck pediment. The dial is engraved on a single sheet of brass (unlike the English practice with separate chapter-ring), with simplified Rococo scrolling and leaf designs, originally intended to be silvered overall. A final note on Burnap is to record that one of his apprentices, in the 1790s, was Eli Terry (1772–1852) who was later to become one of the foremost manufacturers of American clocks, and who was to change the course of domestic horological history.

Before examining the work of Eli Terry we must turn to a famous family of Massachusetts clockmakers, the Willards. The oldest brother of this family was called Benjamin, who was born in Grafton, Massachusetts in 1743, and after his apprenticeship to another famous clockmaker, Benjamin Cheney, taught his brothers Simon, Ephraim and Aaron the art of clockmaking. To the brothers Simon (1753–1848) and Aaron (1757–1844), working at their manufactory at Roxbury, near Boston, we owe the introduction of the first unique American design of clock which is popularly known as the banjo clock, so-named because of its resemblance in profile to that musical instrument. The term 'banjo' is relatively recent since the banjo did not become a popular instrument until the second half of the 19th century, and the Willards called their clock the 'patent timepiece' following their patenting of the design in 1802.

One of the most charming of designs of wall clock ever produced, the banjo clock owes a great deal to French influence, from the gilded Imperial eagle on the top of the case, the contrasting use of polished brass mounts, gilded and polished mahogany, to the gilded and painted glass 'tablets' depicting either topographical scenes, patriotic symbols,

American tall clock signed by Daniel Burnap; this clock was made for his own use; about 1795. *Wadsworth Atheneum, Hartford, Connecticut*

American wall clock, popularly known as a 'banjo' clock; the figures on the tablet below represent Liberty and Justice; signed 'Willard's Patent'; 1802–10. *Yale University Art Gallery, Mabel Brady Garvan Collection*

mythological subjects or floral and geometric ornament. Here French influence, to some extent modified by English elements of Sheraton style, has been married to a newly emerging culture, and ideas derived from French Empire styles is not surprising, for there was much sympathy with the French political cause at the time. The American people had freed themselves from the domination of the English crown, and the French peasantry and lower middle classes had also freed themselves from the despotic rule of the aristocracy. Even more French in feeling is the elaborate form of banjo clock known as the girandole, profusely gilded with its bezel and base surrounded by gilded beads or balls such as were popular on French Empire convex mirror frames, terminating below with a so-called 'bracket' of carved acanthus leaves. Like many weight-powered Continental clocks, the pendulum was hung in front of the movement proper, and a clear aperture was sometimes left in the lower tablet to display the movement of the polished brass bob.

Another distinctive type of early American clock was the Massachusetts shelf clock, a rare design, now highly prized by American collectors. As the manufacture of springs was extremely difficult in the early years of American clockmaking, and even more difficult to replace if broken, dependence on the power of falling weights was a necessity, and continued so until the metallurgical industries of Connecticut made important changes in the second half of the 19th century. To house the weights, the Massachusetts shelf clock was designed like an English bracket clock, but raised on a high wooden plinth, its final form being something of a hybrid between a longcase and a bracket clock. In the example depicted, there is a painted dial and bracket feet of English derivation, and a kidney-shaped aperture for the dial which is distinctively French. It is the almost naïve way in which these foreign influences come together in American furniture that gives early American clocks their special appeal and charm.

Yet one more early American type must be included before returning to the European birthplace of clock styles and fashion, to that perhaps most beautiful American clock of all, the pillar and scroll. The design of this clock has been linked particularly to Daniel Burnap's famous apprentice Eli Terry. However, it should be emphasised that Terry was only responsible for designing and making the movements for this type of clock, and in so doing he was one of the first in America to begin clockmaking on a mass-production basis, using standard jigs and repetition tools driven by water-power at his factory at Northbury, Connecticut (now called Plymouth). In 1806 he contracted to supply 4000 clock movements to Edward and Levi Porter of Waterbury, the deal being completed in two years. These movements were entirely made of wood apart from the pivots, escape wheels, anchor pendulum and a few minor detents and springs. In due course these wooden movements (following a south German country tradition) became more or less standardised units, the wheels and pinions being made of apple and other fruit woods, and the movement plates of oak. The rapidly increasing number of fashionable New England clapboard, Georgian proportioned houses with elegant fireplaces and overmantels, called for narrow and elegant clocks to stand upon them. The pillar and scroll type evolved to fill the need, fitted at first with Terry movements and later with those of other manufacturers.

The design of the pillar and scroll clock, introduced about 1817, relied on the European tradition, but modified by American inventiveness and taste. The prevailing influence is English rather than French. The tall and extremely slender side pillars (of elongated Roman Tuscan derivation), the triple set of gilded urn-shaped spires, the high and simple swan's neck pediment and the convoluted apron front are all an interpretation of the Hepplewhite manner which dominated English fashionable furniture design in the closing years of the 18th century. George Hepplewhite (*d* 1786) was apprenticed to the famous firm of Gillows in Lancaster and later ran his own workshop in Redcross Street, Cripplegate, London. He evolved a delicate, refined and slender style of furniture based on a Neo-Classical foundation but putting stress on the elongated and extremely thin structural members such as chair legs and rails, and emphasising such features as the oval and urn-shaped shield for chair backs and fire-screens. The pattern book which brought him fame was *The Cabinet-Maker and Upholsterer's Guide* which was published by his widow in 1788, two years after his death. No piece of Hepplewhite furniture can be related exactly to the pillar and scroll clock; rather it is the influence of his designs which reflect the taste of London in the closing years of the 18th century, to be picked up with about 20 years' delay, and re-born amongst the enterprising and successful better-off citizens of England's former colony.

The dials of pillar and scroll clocks were made of wood, prepared with gesso and painted, with numerals in arabic or Roman style, and spandrels painted with either flowers or formal ornament. These dials followed, if not closely at least in spirit, the style of white painted iron dials of English longcase clocks of their declining years in the first quarter of the 19th century. The painted glass tablet below the dial gives the clock its special charm and homely appeal, with landscapes, townscapes, floral arrangements, picturesque views, and a little oval aperture to see the pendulum bob. On the interior of the back-board of the case, clearly seen when the door was opened, a printed label gave details of the manufacturer's name, a fashion which was to persist in American clocks until the beginning of the 20th century. In their choice of typefaces and general ornamental arrangement these early labels too have charm and quality, like early theatre playbills or gravestone inscriptions, where the styles of lettering used are varied and mixed, rich in graphic imagery.

Thousands of pillar and scroll clocks were made by many American firms until the late 1820s, but never for the European market. It is said that the rigours of the Atlantic crossing would have caused damage through dampness to the wooden movements, but it is far more likely that the style of case would have appeared somewhat crude to the upper middle classes of England and France, out of date and not suitable for the drawing rooms of London or Paris where there were thriving clockmaking trades. It was the later, very cheap brass movement clocks of the middle and late 19th century which were to be exported in vast numbers to Europe, and neither the pillar and scroll nor the banjo clock belonged to this era of American clockmaking.

By 1830 the American pillar and scroll had declined to make way for other types of narrow shelf clock such as the New Hampshire looking-glass clock, the Empire style clock, the cornice and column clock, the carved column clock, the bronzed looking-glass clock and the stencilled column clock. These various types of clock cases were a natural development from the primary composition of pediment and flanking columns of the pillar and scroll case, the overall form being a basic rectangular box of shallow depth, comfortably to fit on a narrow mantel shelf. The Empire style, or what is sometimes called the 'transitional' style of clock, takes us into the period dealt with in the following chapter. Its general proportion and arrangement, although vastly different in quality of materials and finesse of finish, is not so far

American wall clock known as a 'lyre' clock which is a variation on the 'banjo' theme; carved mahogany with painted dial and painted and gilded tablet; maker unknown; about 1830. *American Clock and Watch Museum, Bristol, Connecticut*

American mantel clock known as a Massachusetts shelf clock; painted, kidney-shaped dial signed Aaron Willard, Boston. The movement and dial date from about 1800 but the case is a later reproduction of the original design. *American Clock and Watch Museum, Bristol, Connecticut*

removed from the French style which inspired it, and which takes us to France where the 'Empire style' was born.

The Empire period in France dates from about 1800 and in terms of furnishing styles can be said to extend to the end of the reign of Charles X in 1830. Strictly speaking, the Empire period began with the coronation of Napoleon as Emperor in 1804. From 1804 to 1814 the French Empire under Napoleon's command was one of continued European warfare, only to be ended by his disastrous retreat from Moscow in 1812, his abdication in 1814 and his final return to France and defeat at Waterloo in 1815. Clockmaking had suffered during the troubled times of the Revolution between 1789 and 1792, but the government of the Directory (1795–99) took steps to revive the making of clocks along with other manufactures, to encourage movement making at Besançon and Grenoble, to establish complex clockmaking at Versailles (which never took off) and to re-build the trade in Paris itself. During Napoleon's consulate from 1799 to 1804 and also during his reign as Emperor, clockmaking—and especially its important adjunct clock casemaking—flourished once more. As in the period of Louis XVI the range of French clock case styles is vast, and for convenience the complete period of about 1800 to 1830 is entitled 'Empire' because the styles of clock design did not significantly begin to change until after the accession of Louis-Philippe in 1830.

Of all the materials used in the cases of decorative 'drawing-room' French clocks of the early 19th century, richly gilded matt bronze is the most characteristic, with parts of the gilding brightly burnished to contrast with the matt finish of the neighbouring areas. This can be seen in the clock of about 1825–30, which may be compared with the American 'Empire' style. This is a portico clock (see p. 101) in which the movement and dial are supported beneath an architrave mounted on four classical columns, in which the necking bands below the capitals and above the bases, and parts of the feet shine brightly, as does the back of the architrave, base and pendulum bob where they will be seen reflected in a mantelpiece mirror. The simplicity and architectural elegance of this clock suggests something of the serene, or perhaps even cold, architectural pre-occupation of the Empire style with the republican virtues of ancient Greece and Rome. This can be seen again in a rare design known as an orrery clock, made by Raingo Frères of Paris at about the same time as the portico clock. An orrery is the name given to a model of the solar system in which the rotation of the Earth round the Sun, and the Moon round the Earth, is either driven by clockwork at precisely the same rate as occurs in nature, or more quickly by hand for demonstration purposes. The name orrery is derived from an original model made by John Rowley about 1713 for Charles Boyle, fourth Earl of Orrery. Interesting as this orrery clock is from a technical point of view, its glory is also in its sumptuous case, arranged as a more elaborate form of portico clock. The orrery mechanism is mounted above the architrave and the movement supported below, the whole mounted on four fluted Corinthian columns between each of which four figures represent the four seasons of the year, relating to the annual calendar scale of the orrery above. Of superlative quality the figures on this clock, in classical garb and of graceful stature, are typical of thousands of modelled and cast figures which ornament French clocks of the Empire period. In their impeccable treatment they remind one of the highly finished classical paintings of Jacques-Louis David (1748–1825), or more particularly his pupil Jean-Auguste-Dominique Ingres (1780–1867), both of whom were champions of Classicism in French art against the growing Romantic movement of the 19th century. The

Greek hair styles and flowing chitons with which these ladies are draped remind one too of the flimsy muslin or linen dresses with their high waists, in Greek fashion, which the elegant women of the Empire period wore, both in England and in France.

Classical figures, in a variety of postures, from one involved in serious intellectual pursuit on a clock from the Bowes Museum in County Durham, to another in bacchanalian abandon at the Lady Lever Art Gallery in Port Sunlight, are representative of those to be found on French figure clocks of the Empire. They are highly finished in matt or burnished gold, and posed in association with miniature furniture and other accoutrements. In both examples the prevailing taste is Greek. In the Bowes Museum clock the young lady in classical dress sits reading on a Greek-style chair with a bust of Homer on a plinth behind, and an eagle appears on a tripod stand beside the table, with a lamp suspended from its beak to light the scene. The whole design exemplified and encouraged the taste for the study of Greek philosophy and thought. The bacchanalian clock at Port Sunlight, exhibited in a replica of Napoleon's bedroom, depicts a recumbent, almost nude figure paying homage to wine, a large bunch of grapes held ecstatically above her

Above left
American mantel clock known as a 'pillar and scroll' clock; the label inside describes it as being 'made and sold at Plymouth, Connecticut'; painted dial with painted glass tablet; Eli Terry & Sons; about 1825

Above right
American mantel clock with a case known as a 'stencilled column and top splat' type; the seconds hand on the painted dial does not indicate true seconds; labelled Eli Terry & Sons, Plymouth, Connecticut; about 1830

Orrery clock in a case of gilded bronze
with figures between the Corinthian
columns representing the seasons;
originally protected by a glass dome;
signed Raingo Frères à Paris; about
1825. *City Museum, Sheffield*

French Empire clock in gilded and patinated bronze; the lamp which hung from the eagle is missing and the minute hand is broken. This superb case was designed by Antoine Ravrio, about 1810. *The Bowes Museum, Barnard Castle, Co. Durham*

French Empire mantel clock in gilded and patinated bronze, mounted on a dark red marble base; clock movement signed Vaillant à Paris; about 1800. *Lady Lever Art Gallery, Port Sunlight*

Left
Mantel régulateur in a glazed, ebonised wooden case; enamelled dials indicating the equation of time, sunrise and sunset, date, day, month; signed Antide Janvier; 1810–20. *Musée des Beaux Arts, Besançon*

Right
French mantel clock in a 'portico' case; decimal dial with an inner twenty-four hour dial; signed Pierre Daniel Destigny, Rouen; about 1825. *Fitzwilliam Museum Cambridge*

French mantel clock known as a 'plate glass' or 'transparent' clock; the movement is supported by a plate of polished glass; no maker's mark; about 1810. *Plas Newydd, Anglesey. Courtesy of the National Trust*

head. In a posture similar to David's famous painting of Mme Récamier (the 'queen' of a salon of literary and political celebrities), or Ingres' painting 'Odalisque', (though far more abandoned than either of these) she lies on a Greek couch or 'squab' with honeysuckle designs from Greek friezes lining the edges, Greek vases at her feet and lions in relief gorging themselves from grape-filled baskets on the side of the plinth. A number of French clocks show negro figures, or American Indians, in a strange and somewhat confused reference to the ideas derived from explorations in Africa and the westward moves of population in North America. Perhaps, too, the current interest in the problems of the emancipation of slavery are to be found in these figure clocks, while there is clearly an allusion to the idea of the 'Noble Savage' and the belief in education through Nature as expressed in Jean-Jacques Rousseau's *Émile* published many years earlier in 1762.

In contrast to the highly decorative 'salon' clocks of France in the Empire period there was the continuing evolution of that superb type of highly scientific and accurate clock, the régulateur, sometimes in long-case and sometimes as a mantel version, but always with a temperature compensated pendulum with its characteristic grid-iron of brass and steel rods and a large circular bob. A mantel régulateur by the great French horologist Antide Janvier (1751–1835) is shown with a set of six dials, of some complexity. Janvier was one of the leading Parisian makers who, in an active life first as an official 'horloger du roi' imprisoned during the Revolution, was later adviser to the Revolutionary government on the subject of decimal time, which was ordered to be introduced in 1793. This new timekeeping method attempted, as with other decimal measurements, to utilise basic standard divisions of ten, and to divide the day into ten hours with 100 minutes for each hour. The system lapsed in Napoleon's time but had never really become popular, so that today decimal dial clocks are extremely rare. Janvier's multiple dialled régulateur shows the equation of time, mean time, times of sunrise and sunset throughout the year and the Zodiacal calendar sign and the date. Its multiple dials were not only a symptom of the desire for showing maximum information of a scientific nature, but were part of that element of showmanship which is characteristic of decorative French clocks, none more so than a clock of about 1825 now in the Time Museum at Rockford, Illinois. Its dials showing time, date, month, signs of the Zodiac and phases of the Moon are splendidly arranged on a large but shallow gilded bronze frame mounted on a marble base. The clock is crowned with a basket of leaves, fruit, pine cones and wheat (symbolic of plenty) and is flanked by two oppositely matching figures of the goddess Diana with arrows in their hands and crescent moons in their hair. This clock has a visible movement which defines it almost as a *pendule squelette* or skeleton clock, of which many were beginning to appear in France at the end of the 18th and beginning of the 19th century. An idea popular later in Victorian England, the French skeleton clock nowhere has a more attractive appeal than in its most simple version known as the plate glass clock or sometimes called the transparent clock. Shorn of all decorative detail apart from the pendulum bob, the frame of the clock is a plain piece of round-arched and polished plate glass into which the front pivots of the wheel train are fitted, powered by a central spring barrel through an enormous yet extremely delicate great wheel. The appeal of the clock is in its clear exposition of its manner of working, uncluttered and dignified in its proportions and thoroughly legible through its moon, or Breguet, hands on the white enamelled chapter ring. The extraordinary contrast

Above
Regulator in mahogany with 'Egyptian' emphasis in its design of tapering case; dial signed Jones, Gray and Co, Liverpool; movement signed James Condliff, Liverpool; about 1830.

Left
French mantel clock of skeleton design, in gilded bronze with enamelled copper dials; the dials were painted by Jean Coteau, indicating above the four seasons, signs of the Zodiac on the main dial, date and month on inner dials, phases of the Moon below; movement unsigned; about 1810. *Courtesy of The Time Museum, Rockford, Illinois*

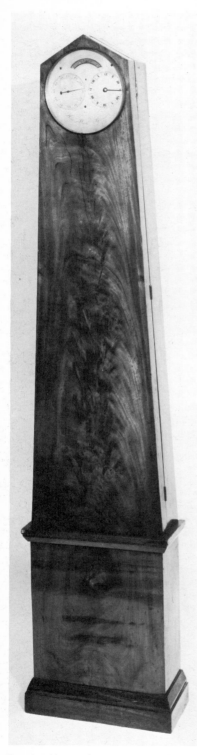

Regulator in a mahogany veneered case
of obelisk form; this precision instrument
has a movement of great simplicity and
originality; signed Henry Ward,
Blandford; about 1810. *British Museum,
London*

between the functional, scientific, superbly made horological machines
of early 19th century France, and the equally superbly made decorative
'salon' clocks with symbolic and anecdotal figure groups, brought
French clockmaking to the highest rank of European art in its day.

The elaborate case styles of the Empire in France did not seriously
influence the design and manufacture of English clock cases, though
many French clocks were bought for use in English interiors, as may be
seen by visiting almost any large English country house. Paris then, as it
had been in the 18th century, remained the centre of the world of
fashion, not only for ladies' dresses but for much in interior and furniture design. By the time Thomas Sheraton's *The Cabinet Dictionary* had
been published in London in 1803 the Grecian style was making its
mark, and Sheraton's book contains pictures of Grecian dining tables,
couches and beds. In England the name given to the period contemporary with the Empire in France is the Regency.

The term Regency refers to the period between 1811 and 1820 when
the future king George IV was the Prince Regent in his father's incapaci-
tated and declining years, but it is rather loosely used to describe the
Greek revival style from about 1800 to about 1830, the time of George
IV's death. In the present context it should not be thought of as being
synonymous with the taste of the Prince Regent himself. The published
works of two important designers in this period introduced new
fashions to England, both books appearing at almost exactly the same
time. The first was by the scholar/architect Thomas Hope (*c* 1770–
1831) who published a book of designs in 1807 under the title of
Household Furniture and Decoration, and the second was George Smith
whose book *A Collection of Designs for Household Furniture and Interior
Decoration* came out in 1808. Although these books were highly influential in spreading the new fashions, neither contained any design for
clock cases, leaving the fashionable London clock casemaking trade to
contrive their designs in the latest fashions as best they could. It is
virtually certain that clocks were ignored by these designers because of
the ready availability of fine French clocks of Empire style, which
would harmonise to perfection with Regency Grecian modes.

Although Greek revival designs were the strongest influence during
the Regency, with some admixture of Roman detail, Egyptian fashions
were strong too, inspired by Napoleon's conquests in Egypt and Syria
at the end of the 18th century. The Director-General of French
museums at the time of the First Empire, Dominique-Vivant Denon,
accompanied Napoleon on his Egyptian campaign of 1798–1801 and in
1802 published an illustrated account called *Voyage dans la Basse et Haute
Égypte* which inspired both French and English designers to introduce
Egyptian motifs such as the sphinx, the winged lion, or the Egyptian
head. The effect of this on English clock design was marginal, but one
particular form of Egyptian architectural style may be seen in the
ubiquitous use of the obelisk shape, in public monuments, memorials
and mantelpiece ornaments. The tall, tapering form of the obelisk was
ideal in providing the basic shape of case for a regulator. Two are
illustrated, a regulator by Condliff of Liverpool (signed on the dial
Jones, Gray & Co) which also has traces of Greek design in the flanking
acroteria on the top of the hood, and the remarkable clock by Henry
Ward of Blandford, Dorset, in a tapering case of great simplicity. The
upward tapering or sloping sides of Egyptian-inspired regulator cases
coincides with the introduction of tapering plates in clock movements
which were popular throughout the first half of the 19th century.

A Greek style mantel clock by Coleman and Chapman of Liverpool,
dating from about 1825 introduces us to a typical English form of the

Right
Mantel clock at 20 St James's Square, London; case of marble set with Wedgwood medallions and gilded bronze mounts incorporating an oak and mistletoe garland, trophies of arms, pineapple finials and a Vitruvian scroll on the base; French movement; about 1790

Below left
Mantel clock in marble and gilded bronze, known as the 'Titus Clock' since it depicts the Roman Emperor Titus in his toga; designed by Matthew Boulton in 1771; French movement by Caillard. *Courtesy of Birmingham Museums and Art Gallery*

Below right
French mantel clock, known as a portico clock; highly finished Roman Tuscan columns and entablature in matt and burnished gilding; enamelled chapter ring; engine-turned centre dial; grid-iron compensated pendulum; maker unknown; 1825–30

Regency period. The case is known as a chamfer-top, its low-pitched angle and strong horizontal emphasis of cornice mouldings being Greek in inspiration, as are the ringed lions' heads forming carrying handles at the sides, and the fluted mouldings at the top and base. Essentially a mantel clock it no longer has a top carrying handle, and the plain white circular dial has supplanted the square or break-arch dial with applied spandrel frets, while a trace of early Renaissance lingers in the form of the pineapple finial. Most important of all in this classical clock is the use of brass inlay as a form of ornament, sunk into the black ebonised wood against which the yellow metal contrasts well. Brass inlays and stringing are features which characterised much furniture of the Regency period, and continued into early Victorian times. It has been suggested that the relative simplicity of Regency furniture in the use of inlaid brass, rather than using expensive inlaid woods which had earlier been favoured by Thomas Sheraton, was the result of a lack of both skilled labour and money during the closing years of the Napoleonic wars and the period immediately following.

The fashionable high quality clock by Coleman and Chapman shows the attempt of a casemaker to keep in touch with the latest fashions in other types of furniture. But the conservative tradition, particularly in provincial regions of the country, continued to produce clock designs which owe their basic forms to the 18th century, retaining features long since abandoned by the fashionable and élite. The traditional English longcase, for example, continued to survive until well into the 19th century, in the northern counties often in an incredibly fat and ugly form, but in other areas retaining the dignity of their Georgian proportions. A clock in a fine mahogany case by J. P. Saddleton of King's Lynn, Norfolk, with break-arch painted dial, may be dated to as late as 1820–30, and this case has the rare virtue of a casemaker's label pasted inside. The maker concerned was Charles Oliver of Spalding in the neighbouring county of Lincolnshire, about 25 miles from Lynn. This would suggest that Oliver was a specialist casemaker to the towns and villages for miles around Spalding, and another clock has been discovered with an Oliver label.

A longcase clock in the English tradition, made in the north-west town of Rochdale about 1805 and of ample proportions, has a painted dial of particular interest in the horological dialogue between England and France, for it contains historical allusions concerned with those two countries. The clock has a musical movement with four religious tunes played on eight bells, selected at will from the subsidiary dial on the front. The four corners of the dial are of seasonal reference, showing courtship for spring, haymaking for summer, harvesting for autumn and a domestic fireside scene for winter. The centre is entirely painted with a scene symbolising the Treaty of Amiens, signed by Lord Cornwallis with Joseph Bonaparte (Napoleon's brother) at Amiens in March 1802, inaugurating a briefly held peace between England and France. That such a dial was not unique is shown by exactly the same design on another Lancashire clock in the same collection, a clock by Houlbrook of Liverpool, with an oval cartouche for the maker's name where the tune selector on the Rochdale clock is placed. Although French inspiration of a sort is found on the painting of this dial, how far removed from contemporary French mantel clocks of the Empire period do these provincial English examples appear!

While the longcase clock was in its final decline in the Regency period, another type of clock was taking its place—the wall or dial clock—which rapidly developed as the changing ways of life of the 19th century replaced those of the previous era. The wall hanging clock is a

Mantel clock of ebonised wood with brass inlay decoration; gilded bronze finial and side handles; signed Coleman and Chapman, Liverpool; about 1825. *Merseyside County Museums, Liverpool*

Opposite page
Automata dial from an organ clock; gilded bronze mounts; signed George Pyke, London; about 1765. *Temple Newsam House, Leeds*

Trade label pasted inside the longcase
clock by J. P. Saddleton

Longcase clock in a mahogany veneered
case with typical East Anglian cresting
above the hood; painted dial; signed
J. P. Saddleton, Lynn; 1820–30

modified form of longcase, known as the tavern clock with a large
circular or octagonal dial and trunk below to accommodate the weights
and long pendulum, sometimes lacquered in the oriental manner and
sometimes ebonised with gilded ornament. It had developed from the
black-dialled wall clock of the 1720s, and in the middle of the 18th
century was frequently to be seen in places of public gathering such as
churches, coaching stations, and as the name suggests in taverns. By the
Regency period these very large clocks had been modified to a smaller
size, used in increasing numbers in coffee houses, inns, clubs and other
public places, and also in the kitchens of country houses, for these
wall-hanging clocks were not for the salon or drawing room. Because
of the appendage below the dial they are known as drop dial or trunk
dial clocks, the former term being largely applied to American
examples of this design. A coloured etching by Thomas Rowlandson
(1756–1827) of a London coffee house shows a trunk dial clock, hanging
on the wall amongst the hats of the robust diners who are seated in the
screened-off cubicles. This clock is something of a transitional type
between the tavern clock and the later trunk dial, but with its horizontal
scroll moulding to the bottom of the trunk suggests a date of about 1800
to 1810. The trunk dial became extremely popular in the 19th century,
with American and German versions too, but its somewhat staid and
restrained features were rarely to be seen in France.

By the end of the period under discussion styles were changing yet
again, and during the reigns of George IV (1820–30) and William IV
(1830–37) new influences were at work leading to revivals of earlier
styles in the middle of the 19th century. A mantel clock of 1825–30 by
the famous makers of quality clocks, Litherland, Davies & Co of
Liverpool, points us in this direction. At first glance the clock is pure
Gothic revival, with cusped dial aperture and o-gee shaped door, with
pointed finials, off-set buttresses and a steeply pointed gable front. But
the brass inlay, the ball feet and the fluted lower moulding remind us of
the Regency style, like the inlaid ebonised clock by Cole & Chapman
from the same town. The dial centre is engine-turned, of fine quality
like those of the portico clocks of the French Empire. The lettering
engraved on the silvered dial plate reminds us of the varieties of typo-
graphical styles found on American printed clock labels, and it stresses
the importance of the commercial exploitation of a name on the most
looked-at part of the clock.

Painted dial from a longcase musical
clock with a centrepiece symbolising the
Treaty of Amiens; corner paintings of the
seasons; signed John Barnish,
Rochdale; 1805–10. *Stuart Hall
Collection*

Coloured etching of a scene in a London
coffee house by Thomas Rowlandson
(1756–1827); 1800–10

Above left
Mantel clock in mahogany with brass inlays in the pinnacles; the Gothic revival forms are mixed with Regency elements; silvered dial-plate, enamelled chapter ring, engine-turned centre; signed Litherland Davies and Co. Liverpool; about 1825–30. *Merseyside County Museums, Liverpool*

Above right
Mantel clock known as a 'Pendule Sympathique' with Boulle-type marquetry and gilded bronze ornament; a watch made to work with the clock was placed in the holder above at night when the clock wound it and set it to time; completed in 1835 for the Duc d'Orleans, son of the King of France; made by Abraham-Louis Breguet. *Courtesy of The Time Museum, Rockford, Illinois*

This chapter cannot end without mention of one of the most remarkable clocks ever made, close in date to the clock by Litherland and Davies, and from the workshop of one of the world's most famous and possibly greatest clock and watchmakers, Abraham-Louis Breguet (1747–1823). Breguet was born at Neuchâtel and came to Paris at 18 years of age to apprentice himself to various outstanding horologists, also to study mathematics and physics. After establishing a workshop in the Quai de l'Horloge in partnership with Xavier Gide, he quickly assembled a wide and wealthy clientèle for his products amongst the aristocracy of Europe. Apart from his absence from Paris during the Revolution and subsequent Terror, he remained there for the rest of his life. The house of Breguet became justly famous with men of the highest rank and his workshops were employing about 100 skilled workmen at the beginning of the Empire period. Like most successful manufacturers he was not only a superb artist and craftsman, but he was also a man of keen business and commercial sense. In 1807 Abraham-Louis took into partnership his son Antoine-Louis and the firm became known as Breguet & Fils, later to be the Breguet Neveu Compagnie. In its founder's own lifetime, and after his death, the company was responsible for many extremely important horological inventions and attained a level of quality in its clocks and watches which has never been surpassed.

The Breguet clock illustrated is one of the horological superlatives of all time, known as a pendule sympathique. Although Breguet had first conceived the idea as early as 1795, almost certainly for reasons of commercial promotion rather than as a contribution to the science of horology, and made several before his death, the pendule sympathique shown was made in 1835 for the Duc d'Orléans, pretender to the throne of France. It is housed in a gilded bronze case, decorated with Boulle-type marquetry which is reminiscent of designs of 150 years earlier. The clock is an eight-day, quarter-striking instrument and its extraordinary feature is that it has a cradle above into which a specially constructed pocket watch could be placed which the clock wound up and set to correct time every night, while its owner was in bed. To quote George Daniels, the leading authority on the work of Breguet, 'The sympathique is a jewel of misplaced ingenuity in a forest of scientific horological endeavours, and their very existence is sufficient reason for their manufacture, for they never cease to amaze and mystify' (from *The Art of Breguet*, 1977 by George Daniels).

Something of the flavour and sentiment of the Regency period in England, or the Empire period in France, may be felt in a little poem first published in 1807 by one Charlotte Smith, addressed to a young lady on seeing a magnificent French timepiece at the house of an acquaintance[1]:

For her who owns this splendid toy,
*   Where use with elegance unites,*
Still may its index point to joy,
*   And moments wing'd with new delights.*

Sweet may resound each silver bell,—
*   And never quick returning chime,*
Seem in reproving notes to tell,
*   Of hours mispent, and murder'd time.*

Tho' Fortune, Emily, deny
*   To us these splendid works of art,*
The woods, the lawns, the heaths supply
*   Lessons from nature to the heart.*

In every copse, and shelter'd dell,
*   Unveil'd to the observant eye,*
Are faithful monitors, who tell
*   How pass the hours and seasons by.*

The green-robed children of the spring
*   Will mark the periods as they pass,*
Mingle with leaves time's feather'd wing,
*   And bind with flowers his silent glass.*

[1] Originally published in the *Annual Register*, 1807, and quoted by E. J. Wood in *Curiosities of Clocks & Watches*, London 1866.

ART AND INDUSTRY: I
Gothic and other Revivals

The Great Exhibition of the Works of Industry of all Nations, 1851, held in Joseph Paxton's magnificent glass building in Hyde Park, London, subsequently christened 'The Crystal Palace', was an event of immense importance in the middle of the 19th century. It not only gave tangible expression to the self-confidence of England—the leading industrial nation of the world at that time—but it also left detailed accounts and illustrated catalogues, critical articles and clear expressions of the achievements of that age in such quantities that the event can be considered as a 'touch stone', enabling us to assess the standards of taste which were prevalent in those days. Bearing in mind the fact that all the objects assembled together for the exhibition were specially selected as being outstanding in their class, such objects cannot be accepted as being altogether typical of everything that was made at the time. At least they give us an idea not only of the incredible advances that had taken place in engineering, the pure sciences, manufacturing techniques and the growth of industrial power, but they also provide examples of the sheer confusion into which the whole process of designing objects of everyday use had fallen. One of the most important commentators on the domestic objects in the exhibition, Ralph Nicholas Wornum (1812–77), Lecturer on Art at the Government School of Design and Keeper of the National Gallery, wrote a paper which was published in the Art Journal Illustrated Catalogue of the exhibition, entitled *The Exhibition as a Lesson in Taste*, in which he attempted to analyse the categories of ornament into which the decoration of the objects displayed could be placed. Altogether Wornum considered that there were nine different styles, three antique, three mediaeval and three modern. The 'antique' styles he labelled Egyptian, Greek and Roman; the 'mediaeval' styles Byzantine, Saracenic and Gothic; the 'modern' styles Renaissance, Cinquecento (Italian art of the 16th century) and Louis Quatorze. Within these general headings he went on to explain exactly what he meant by these periods of ornament, leaving the modern reader not a little confused, though it is clear in the end that the Renaissance and Cinquecento were the styles most employed by the best European designers.

A casual glance through the pages of the illustrated exhibition catalogue, with its vast range of wood-block prints of objects in the most elaborate styles imaginable, leads us to consider why the 19th century should have brought forth such a confusion of styles, whereas in the past each new style had naturally evolved from its predecessor according to architectural precedent, mastery of materials and the prevailing spirit of the age. The answer to this must lie in the fact that industrial and scientific progress had been so sudden, had upset the basic structure and pattern of urban and agrarian life, had introduced new systems of communication and transport, had changed the very social fabric of society itself, that artists and designers fell back upon historical forms of ornament and design because they had no means of evolving a new set of standards to meet the challenge of their times. That new sets

Opposite page
Page 117 from the *Art Journal Illustrated Catalogue of The Industry of all Nations*; 1851

The silver manufactures of Mr. M. EMANUEL, of London, evince great taste in design, and some very excellent workmanship. He exhibits a variety of objects besides those we have here engraved, such as gilt candelabra, gilt plateau,

with china racks and medallions, processes of gold manufacture. The first we introduce is one of a pair of rock crystal CANDLESTICKS,

silver, and gilt, with figures of children, sea-horses, and marine objects, composing the base. The next is a FLOWER-VASE, of richly coloured glass, mounted in silver; the handles are made to represent boys climbing upwards to the

flower stems, and the pedestal is composed of groups of figures and horses. The two objects commencing the other columns are silver DESSERT STANDS. The vine forms their stems, at the

base of which children are at play with animals; the dishes are supported by a sort of trellis-work of the leaves and fruit of the vine. But the

attributes; and, surmounting the top, is Phœbus driving the chariot of the sun; the composition of this group is full of spirit, and the whole of

most important contribution of this manufacturer is a large silver CLOCK, designed by Mr. Woodington, the well-known sculptor: it is truly a fine work of art. Between four figures,

indicating the "Seasons," is one of "Time," in the attitude of repose; above the dial is a bas relief, representing the winds and their various

the figures are exceedingly well modelled. Mr. Emanuel has done wisely in securing the services of an artist of acknowledged talent and repute.

of standards were being evolved through the ideas of the engineers we can, with hindsight, now understand. The designer of the Crystal Palace itself, Joseph Paxton (1801–65) had created a new concept in the organisation and lighting of space and in constructional techniques of pre-fabrication. The railway age which dawned in 1830 had given rise to the construction of stations, bridges, tunnels and other structures of unprecedented scale and proportions, and through the use of iron and steel by such engineers as Isambard Kingdom Brunel (1806–59) new aesthetic ideas were born. A host of other industrial enterprises were changing the world, first in England as the major pioneering industrial nation, but later on a world-wide basis. The world too, through the building and exploitation of colonial empires, was becoming a smaller place, in which cultural, scientific, aesthetic, religious and philosophical ideas were spreading about as never before. Early experiments in the nature of electricity by Alessandro Volta (1745–1827), Humphry Davy (1778–1829), André-Marie Ampère (1775–1836), Michael Faraday (1791–1867), George Simon Ohm (1787–1854) and many others, were leading to new concepts in the understanding of matter, and also to new possibilities of communication such as the electric telegraph, introduced by Sir Charles Wheatstone (1802–75) and W. F. Cooke in 1837. Such were the visionaries of the 19th century who laid the foundations of our present technological society. With hindsight the 'battle of the styles' which raged in the design of municipal buildings and domestic objects of household furnishing seems somewhat irrelevant today compared with the achievements of the engineers and the men of science. The world of 19th-century clockmaking, however, at least as far as the external appearance of clocks was concerned, was in the hands of the furniture and interior designers, who with their eclectic ideas of what was appropriate perpetuated a dependence on the revival of designs from the past.

The 19th century, due to the divisions which had taken place between the arts and the sciences, thus found itself in something of a schizophrenic situation, where the men of science were employing a set of values completely at variance with those of the academic, artistic élite, in exactly the same way as the ideas of that great biologist and botanist, Charles Robert Darwin (1809–82) were at variance with the ideas of the established Church when his major work, *The Origin of Species* was published in 1859. A century and a quarter later we can look back at the dilemmas of that epoch with a view which enhances our admiration for the scientific and engineering pioneers. This view with hindsight now allows us to recognise also the charm, the humanity, the humour, the virtuosity and the undoubted sincerity of the champions of the 'establishment' and their academic endeavours in the world of architecture and interior design.

A man who undoubtedly did much to encourage one of the main 'revival' styles in architecture and furnishing in the 19th century was Augustus Welby Northmore Pugin (1812–52), who is today famous for his Gothic detailing at the Palace of Westminster in London, and as a Roman Catholic convert for his enthusiastic promotion of Gothic ideas. In the 1830s and 1840s he fought for the Gothic style as the only practicable and honest style for the buildings of a Christian nation. He expounded these ideas in his book *The True Principles of Pointed or Christian Architecture* (1841) having already, in 1835, published a book of drawings under the title of *Gothic Furniture of the Style of the Fifteenth Century*. Men such as Pugin influenced the design of the Gothic revival clock by Litherland, Davies & Co., seen in the seventh chapter, and another 'Gothic' mantel clock of about 1835 is shown to illustrate the effect of the 19th century Gothic revival on household clocks of the period. Its foliate finials, pierced side frets and gadrooned mouldings at the top indicate clearly how other styles, however, from a Renaissance past, penetrated the overall design.

An English clock in the Gothic taste of the mid-19th century was the Scott Memorial Clock, inspired by the famous Scott Memorial in Edinburgh with its sculpture by Sir Francis Legatt Chantrey. A number of such 'Scott' skeleton clocks were made, and the pierced brass plates which form their frames, with pointed arches, flying buttresses, buttress offsets and soaring pinnacles remind us of the open frames of real Gothic clocks. Some Gothic mid-Victorian skeleton clocks became so ornate in their representations of the west fronts of great cathedral churches that the very element which should have been the essence of skeleton clocks—that is to be able clearly to see the working parts—was

Mantel clock in the Gothic taste;
veneered in mahogany; silvered dial;
quarter-striking on eight bells; signed
Widenham, London; about 1835

utterly lost in the welter of architectural details. To be able to read the time from these clocks was apparently the last concern of their enthusiastic makers!

The open frames of all skeleton clocks were protected from dust and draughts by a cylindrical domed or parabolic clear glass shade of a type extensively used in Victorian households to protect wax flowers, stuffed birds, biscuit porcelain figures and the like. Many have now perished through careless handling or straight-forward accidents in the weekly routine of removal to wind the clock. These shades at one time were cheap to replace and were made in a great variety of shapes and sizes, from wooden or cast-iron moulds. In England two famous glass makers, Chance Brothers of Birmingham and the St Helens Glass Company (now Pilkington Brothers Limited) retailed ornamental glass shades, but many were purchased from France and Belgium. The advertisement of the importing firm of Claudet & Houghton, from their warehouse at No. 89 High Holborn, London, shows a range of such shades, the central example covering what is probably a French marble clock with a standing figure at the side. Wooden stands in mahogany or rosewood could also be supplied.

These examples of Gothic inspired clocks would not have pleased Pugin half as much as the superb and richly gilded metal-cased clock of the 1850s, described as of 'pyx' form from its resemblance to the box or casket in which the consecrated bread is kept for the Christian communion (see p. 135). Its richly ornamented case set with semi-precious stones linked with beaded and scrolled tendrils, enhanced with flowers and trailing vines picked out with pearls, is in its overall form a Gothic design, but its details are of a mixture of styles. The arcade of pointed arches on the lower plinth are Gothic, as are the quatrefoil roundels on each of the finials. The pierced arcades above and below the clear quartz corner columns are, however, of Romanesque design derived from 11th and 12th-century architecture, while the acanthus leaves round the lowest moulding and the anthemion border ornament on the gable top are Greek. The idea of setting a metal case with large, semi-precious stones owes much to Celtic art, and the scrolled flowers on the main front show a clear influence of the Renaissance style. It is more than possible that this case was made in a Continental workshop, or by foreign craftsmen working in London, and the dial itself, with enamelled plaques with blue Roman numerals and Breguet-type hands has more than a passing resemblance to French design of the 18th century.

The firm of Hunt & Roskell who were responsible for retailing this clock was one of the high class manufacturing gold and silversmithing firms in London in the middle of the 19th century. The *Art Journal Illustrated Catalogue of the Industry of All Nations* had much to say about this company in 1851, of which the following is a quotation:

'Few knowing the vast resources and the long experience of the eminent firm of Messrs Hunt & Roskell of London, who now conduct the business formerly carried on by Messrs Storr & Mortimer, will be surprised to find them making a display in the Exhibition commensurate with the reputation of an establishment that produces many of the most costly manufactured articles in the precious metals. Without disparagement to any other house in London, in a similar branch of business, it may be said that Messrs Hunt & Roskell have no rival in the extent of their transactions, and a visit to their showrooms is like inspecting a museum of Art ... In the remarks we have occasionally made in the *Art-Journal* upon the comparative merits of foreign and English silver-work, it has been stated that the inferiority

Advertisement for the French glass shade importing and retailing warehouse of Claudet and Houghton, London; from the *Manchester Directory*, 1833. *Manchester Public Libraries*

CLAUDET & HOUGHTON,
French Glass Shade & Lamp Shade
WAREHOUSE,
No. 89,
High Holborn.

wn, Sheet, Fluted. Coloured. Painted. Engraved & Ornamented Glass for Windows

Skeleton clock known as a Scott Memorial Clock, its design being based on that monument; unsigned but made by the firm of William Frederick Evans of Handsworth, Birmingham; about 1855. *Courtesy of Derek Roberts Antiques, Tonbridge*

Sir Walter Scott Memorial in Princes Street, Edinburgh, on which the Scott Memorial clock was based. *Courtesy of Phillips in Scotland*

of the latter has been in a great measure attributable to the absence of good designs, and to the superior taste and delicacy of finish in the foreign workmen. Recent political events abroad have, however, brought over a number of the latter to this country, and there cannot be a doubt that we have greatly benefited by this fusion of adventitious aid with English energy, perseverance and capital. Moreover, manufacturers have found it essential to their interests to seek the assistance of other heads than those of the mere artisan, however skilful as a workman, to invent, and suggest, and improve. Hence from these two causes a decided change for the better has, within the past few years, been perceptible in every branch of this department of Industrial Art; and we may add, without egotism, that the pages of the *Art-Journal* have had some influence in effecting this amelioration.'

Mantel clock of black slate; front panel of
pottery decorated in white enamels on a
blue ground; French movement; maker
of case unknown; 1850–60. *Drop Dial
Antiques, Bolton*

In general proportion something like the richly gilded and jewelled
Hunt & Roskell masterpiece, and also like the Gothic structures with
which English cities were well endowed in Victorian times, is another
clock, but this time in black slate or marble with a ceramic front.
Eclecticism in English 19th-century domestic art did not confine itself
to styles alone, but to materials too. Designed for a private study, or
perhaps the lord mayor's parlour in a provincial town hall, this massive
clock with a French movement is of Belgian marble, engraved and
gilded on its sides and plinths with Gothic quatrefoils and a sextfoil
aperture above which dominates, like a French rose window, the centre
of the gable front. Extraordinarily the front of the case is a slab of fired
pottery, cemented to it, on which white enamels contrast with a rich
blue ground. The ornamental style of this design is seen to have Gothic
features woven together in a manner which recalls the Italian Renaissance, painted in a style which can be associated with Italian majolica
pottery.

The far spreading effect of the Gothic revival style was perhaps most
strongly felt in the United States, and it is to that country we must
return before looking at the classical and other styles which had
stronger influence than Gothic on European 19th-century design. In
that marvellous primer for American architects by Andrew Jackson
Downing (1816–52) *The Architecture of Country Houses*, published in
1850, the dependence on European styles for building and interior
design in America is clear, and the spirit of much of what Downing had
to say is summed up in the following quotation:

> 'And as there are, among writers, the dramatic, the serious, the
> narrative, and the didactic styles, each peculiarly adapted to the
> expression of certain modes of thought and life, so there are the
> Grecian, the Italian, the Gothic, the Romanesque, and other styles—
> each peculiarly capable of manifesting certain mental temperaments
> or organisations, or of harmonising with certain tastes in the life of
> the individual.'

It is curious to note that in dealing with interior design and furniture
Downing had nothing to say about clocks, for American clocks of the
mid-19th century were to display the same profusion of revival styles as
in Europe. As far as Gothic is concerned Downing comments:

> 'There has been little attempt made at adapting furniture in this
> (Gothic) style to the more simple Gothic of our villas and country
> houses in America. Yet we are confident that this may be done in such
> a manner as to unite a simple and chaste Gothic style with forms
> adapted to and expressive of our modern domestic life.'

How could Downing write this when two of the most popular of the
many types of American clock, in Gothic versions, had been introduced
by one of the foremost Bristol, Connecticut cabinetmakers, Elias
Ingraham, about 1840, and had become well established in the United
States? According to K. D. Roberts both designs had been marketed
before 1842, and both styles were widely copied by his numerous
competitors. As an architect and interior designer Downing, like the
publishers of pattern books in England such as John Claudius Loudon,
who brought out *An Encyclopaedia of Cottage, Farm and Villa Architecture
and Furniture* in 1833, neglected to include clocks because they were
regarded as a special group of objects, not strictly in the same class as
beds, chairs, tables and so forth, and because they were the products of
specialist manufacturers whose primary concern was the making of the
mechanical parts.

The two versions of American Gothic clocks, the Round Gothic and the Sharp Gothic, known sometimes respectively as the beehive clock and the steeple clock have that same simplification of the European prototype from which they were undoubtedly derived, as had the American tall clock, the banjo clock, and the pillar and scroll clock which were noticed in the previous chapter. The round Gothic is a shelf clock with its top shaped as a simple pointed arch in continuous curves from the upright sides, while the sharp Gothic, or steeple Gothic is either a simple sharp triangular pointed gable or, more commonly, has a pair of flanking pinnacles on each side. Further development of the latter style was the Gothic-on-frame clock in which a lower, wider part

Above left
Villa in the Pointed Style—an illustration from *The Architecture of Country Houses* by Andrew Jackson Downing; published in the USA in 1850

Above right
American mantel clock known as 'Sharp Gothic'; this clock has been adapted as an alarm clock with a braking lever on the top left side; a similarly adapted example has the label *Winward's New 8-day Railway Alarm Clock* pasted inside; Seth Thomas Clock Company; about 1860

Below left
American mantel clock of 'Round Gothic' form; veneered in mahogany; cut and etched glass tablet below; hand-painted iron dial; movement by E. C. Brewster and Co., Bristol, Connecticut; about 1843

Below right
American mantel clock of 'Round Gothic' form, similar to that by E. C. Brewster but with 'rippled' mouldings; these were cut by means of a cutting frame and cam; movement by Jonathan C. Brown, Bristol, Connecticut; about 1848

of the case had its own flanking pinnacles in addition to those on the top. Other variations occurred in which these basic forms were elaborated with stylish mouldings, on the front of the case, giving the clocks the charming name of rippled Gothic.

Whereas the English trade of the 19th century had come to depend for clock movements on a limited number of specialist manufacturers, or on large numbers of imported French, and later German movements, the American factories were based on a different system, that of mass-production of an intensive kind. Mostly based in or near Bristol, Connecticut, many firms such as the Forestville Manufacturing Company, Brewster & Ingrahams, the Litchfield Manufacturing Company, the Ansonia Clock Company and the William L. Gilbert Clock Company

American wall-hanging calendar clock in a veneered rosewood case; Seth Thomas Clock Company; dated 1876

American mantel clock in the 'Empire' style; known also as a 'Column Clock'; paper covered columns in imitation of marble; the upper glass tablet is decorated with the Royal Coat of Arms and the lower with the American Eagle; E. N. Welch Manufacturing Company; about 1860

American mantel clock with facetted top known as an 'Octagon'; New Haven Clock Company; about 1880

Mantel clock fitted with an alarm; a humble American clock known as a 'Cottage' clock; Waterbury Clock Company; about 1880

set up their factories in the 1840s and '50s. They used brass movements whose cheap manufacture had been made possible by the exploitation of specialised tooling and because of the introduction of brass rolling mills at Waterbury. Many of the early movements were of extraordinarily ingenious design, and it is worth noting that in a single year (1849–50) the total number of clocks made by eleven Bristol firms was 187 500. The enormous achievement of 19th-century American Connecticut clockmakers has been reviewed elsewhere (see Bibliography) but the impact on clockmaking in England particularly was in many ways devastating. In 1854 a Liverpool importer of clocks reported that 'American clocks are imported from the United States by almost every vessel, in small boxes containing dozens or half dozens . . . the number of boxes brought to Liverpool last year amounted to upwards of 8,000, and the clocks 60,000, weight 300 tons, value £30,000.' On these figures the actual average cost of each clock was, therefore, ten shillings, a price which in those days no English clockmakers could possibly match. Moreover, American clocks were easy to maintain, extremely reliable even when neglected, and available in a wide range of case styles, of 30-hour or eight-day duration, with or without alarms. The cheap clock for every English working household had finally arrived due to American enterprise, in cases whose design owed much to the very country whose clockmaking business it nearly strangled.

It must be emphasised that Gothic inspired designs for American clock cases were not the only styles used in the mid-19th century. The American 'Empire' clock was still being made in a modified form known as the column clock and an example is shown of this type by the E. N. Welch Manufacturing Company which was founded in 1856 at

German Black Forest mantel clock inspired by the American 'cottage' design; Philip Haas and Söhne; 1870–80

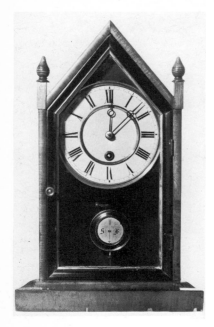

German Black Forest mantel clock inspired by the American 'Sharp Gothic' design; maker unknown; about 1880

Table regulator in veneered mahogany case of elegant architectural design; signed Jump, London; about 1840. *Courtesy of G. E. Marsh, Antique Clocks, Winchester*

Forestville, Connecticut. The designs of its decals (transfer prints) on the glass tablets both proclaim its American origin and suggest its intended destination.

The E. N. Welch column clock has two doors, the upper being decorated with the English Royal Coat of Arms, intended for the English market, in the centre of which is a small oval aperture, left clear to reveal the bob of the pendulum. In this eight-day clock, however, the pendulum is not of the length suggested, for the door is designed to fit a smaller, 30-hour clock. The lower door has a different tablet with a design incorporating the American Eagle, behind which the actual pendulum bob of the clock may be seen. The massive side half-columns giving the name to this type of clock are decorated with marbled graining, and the fat and extremely heavy gilded capitals and bases only bear a passing resemblance to their classical origins, the capitals especially perhaps being vaguely based on Egyptian lotus-bud designs, if on anything at all. The printed label inside the clock has a view of the factory where it was made, to inspire confidence in the solidity and dependability of the concern responsible for it.

The distinctive and unique American calendar clock was first introduced by a patent granted to John H. H. Hawes of Ithaca, New York, on 17 May 1853, marking the advent of what must be one of the most ingenious of American clock types, some of the earliest being made as column clocks by the Seth Thomas Clock Company. Before Seth Thomas's death in 1859 the site of the factory belonging to this company was called Plymouth Hollow in Connecticut, later re-named, appropriately enough, Thomas Town. Calendar clocks were made for business offices, banks and other places where ready indication of the day, date and month was a necessary feature. Expensive and complex calendar clocks had been constructed in England and France in the 18th century, but the triumph of the American calendar clock was the cheapness of its manufacture, the simplicity and ingenuity of its mechanism, and the fact that from a patent granted one year after that of John H. H. Hawes a fully perpetual calendar mechanism came into being, patented on 19 September 1854 by William H. Akins and Joseph C. Burritt, both of Ithaca. By 'fully perpetual' is meant that the mechanism was self-adjusting for the various lengths of the months, including the extra date of 29 February every leap year. The American calendar clock remained popular throughout the 19th century, in most examples the calendar being shown on a separate dial placed below the main clock dial. The day of the week and the month appear in horizontal slots on the left and right of the dial, while the date is indicated by a rotating pointer. Though this type of clock was rarely exported to Europe, there can be little doubt that its development was inspired by French calendar clocks of the Empire period though the problem was solved in a simple and graphic way.

Two other basic forms of American shelf clock owed their origin to the middle years of the 19th century, and both survived to the end of the century in spite of the extraordinary revival of complex Renaissance designs of the 1870s onwards. One is the ubiquitous American o-gee shelf clock (see p. 135) and the other a group of round-headed, triangular-topped, flat-topped or facet-topped, spring-powered mantel clocks known by a wide variety of names such as Sultan (round), Tuscan (triangular), Octagon (facetted) and Cottage (flat) though the range of patented names by many firms is endless. These clocks, of 30-hour or eight-day duration, were spring powered and essentially portable. Their larger contemporaries, the o-gee clocks, were weight-powered, the weights being concealed in the sides of the cases. The o-gee case was so-called because of the o-gee section of the moulding which completely surrounded the front edges, and it is basically the simple form and overall classical proportion of these extremely cheap and popular clocks which gives them their peculiar appeal. In exactly the same way as the American nation continued to use the basic proportions of Georgian architecture in its vernacular building style, so the unpretentious nature of these homely clocks has a universal appeal for those who can appreciate their restful charm, and steady though very audible tick.

The importation of cheap American clocks into Europe in the 19th century was met with consternation by the clockmaking trade, though to judge by contemporary advertisements the retailing agents were doing quite well! German manufacturers, with their background of a Black Forest cottage industry originally making wooden movement clocks, but later of brass, responded to the challenge of American competition and began to make clocks by American methods, sometimes in the American style. A company which included amongst its products clocks of American inspiration was Philipp Haas und Söhne of St Georgen in the Black Forest, which adopted the trademark *Uhrenfabrik Teutonia* in the 1870s on clocks intended for the export market. An example is shown of a 'cottage' clock in which the printed glass tablet is decorated with a symmetrical scrolled design in colours and gold against a black ground, and inside the case, as in American clocks, the trademark of the maker is printed on a label pasted to the back. This may be compared in general form to a true American 'cottage' clock by the Waterbury Clock Company, known in their catalogue as *Cottage No. 2*, utilising a tablet design based loosely on a Greek fret. Another example of an American-inspired German clock of the 1870s is a 'sharp Gothic' clock closely resembling its United States competitors, but with smaller pinnacles, a door at the back (unknown in American examples), and a pendulum clearly visible and simulating a compensated grid-iron type.

English clockmaking and watchmaking in the 19th century suffered severely from the inroads of American enterprise. Later the importation of German clocks, coupled with the ready availability of French drum movements, did not help the English clock movement-making trade either. In the field of high-quality clockwork English workshops still flourished and two examples show the high standards of work which was carried on. Both clocks are precision instruments, distinguished not only by the severely restrained nature of their casework, but also the superb finish of their movements. The first is a mantel or table regulator of about 1840, by the firm of Jump of London, simple and elegant in its arched-top case with glazed 'windows' at the sides and above to reveal the quality of its working parts. In this it is related to the open glazing of French régulateurs, but the clock is otherwise of completely restrained English design with scarcely a reference to past architectural style. Only the fine ovolo mouldings and the turned brass feet, and the perfection of its classical proportions indicate the sound architectural standards on which it is based. The second clock is also a regulator, but of longcase design and like the Jump table regulator with round arched top. The fully glazed case is in ebonised wood with gilded cavetto mouldings, and the magnificent movement is fitted to the case on pierced and cusped brass brackets of Gothic design. The elaborate stand in the base of the trunk to hold the pendulum amplitude scale is of fretted wood and incised gilded lines, tracing a pattern of Greek devices. This clock bears the name of Arnold & Lewis, a high class establishment at one time in the fashionable St Ann's Square, Manchester, and was probably

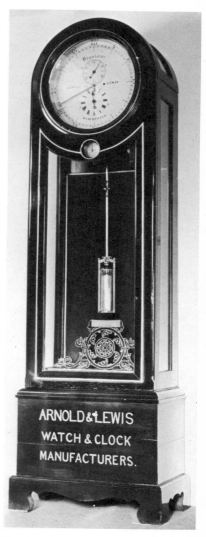

Regulator in an ebonised wooden case with gilded mouldings and lettering; the small subsidiary dial contains the needle of a galvanometer to record telegraphed time signals; the name Arnold and Lewis is that of a high class Manchester retailer; about 1855. *Stuart Hall Collection*

Mantel clock with flanking vases, the clock in the Rococo revival style; the clock is fitted with an electrically controlled 'slave' mechanism, and the terminals may be seen on each side of the base; illustrated from *A Short History of the Electric Clocks, with Explanations of their Principles and Mechanism* by Alexander Bain; 1852

Wall-hanging electrically powered 'master' clock in an oak case of Gothic revival design; signed Alexander Bain, Patentee, No. 235; 1845–50. *Clockmakers' Company Museum, London*

made about 1855. Perhaps its most interesting feature is the small dial beneath the main dial, displaying the needle of a galvanometer. This was used to record exact time signals sent on the telegraph line from Greenwich, via the Post Office telegraph system, for Arnold & Lewis prided themselves on the accuracy of their public time service which was also displayed by means of a time ball on a post outside the shop, synchronised by electrical contacts from the regulator itself.

Experiments in the transmission of time between places far distant from each other using electrical pulses had been undertaken as early as 1846 when Alexander Bain (1810–77) had synchronised two clocks, one in Edinburgh and the other in Glasgow, by means of a telegraph line. Bain's most important contribution, however, to the introduction of electro-mechanical control of clocks was by devising a system in which the pendulum of a clock was impulsed by electro-magnetic means, dispensing with the need for weights or springs and also, more importantly, almost eliminating that most difficult problem in all mechanical clockwork, the interference of friction and the problem of lubrication. Alexander Bain's electric clocks were displayed in the Great Exhibition of 1851, and the example shown is one of his electrical 'master' clocks in a wall-mounted case of Gothic revival design. Here the dichotomy of the engineer and the furniture designer is illustrated to perfection, and perhaps even more so in a domestic 'slave' clock, designed to be electrically controlled from the 'master' clock in another room of the house or public building in which it was installed. Its electrical mechanism is fitted in a richly scrolled, Rococo, French styled case under a glass shade, with electric terminals at the sides and with matching flanking vases. The illustration is taken from Alexander Bain's *A Short History of the Electric Clocks with Explanations of their Principles and Mechanism*, published in London a year after the Great Exhibition, at a time when his brilliant career was to go into a sad decline.

In the middle years of the 19th century the exaggerated use of revival styles in both domestic furniture and the design of buildings, coupled with the increasing ugliness of industrial towns and cities, led a group of young men to react against what was happening. They tried to revive those principles of fine design and true craftsmanship which had been lost, the former through the confusion which existed about what was thought of as 'design' by the established architects, and the latter by the encroachment of mass-production and the tyranny of the factory system. A leading figure in what came to be called the 'Arts and Crafts' movement was William Morris (1834–96) who as well as being an ardent socialist, intent on changing the political system as well as changing the quality of its products, founded a firm in 1861 to produce articles of fine hand-craftsmanship in furniture, textiles and wall-papers. Morris's example, through his designs, his essays and his public lectures caused others to follow, such as Charles Lock Eastlake (1836–1906) who strove to bring ordinary people's attention back to the plain virtues of undecorated furniture of simple and honest construction, and published his views in *Hints on Household Taste* in 1868. Many progressive architects and designers contributed to this movement in the second half of the 19th century, and the last example of an English Gothic clock design in this chapter came from the hand of one of these men, William Burges (1827–81).

It might seem a contradiction in terms to describe and illustrate a Gothic clock case/secrétaire as being from a progressive school of designers, but neither Morris, nor Eastlake, nor Burges nor others at that time were able to throw off the influence of Gothic ideas, as was

Secrétaire cabinet in an individual form of Gothic revival style; painted and gilded wood containing a clock in the upper right corner; William Burges; about 1875. *City Art Gallery, Manchester*

possible in the 20th century. Rather, they attempted to revive sound principles of hand-craftsmanship in which the skills of the craftsman would be honoured and encouraged, in opposition to the mechanical lifelessness of the products of the machine. In working timber, for example, hand sawing, planing and cutting of joints was considered a life-enhancing virtue, just as William Morris found it necessary to spin dye and weave his own textile fabrics, or make his own paper and cast his own type-faces for printing his books. A leading figure in a group of painters who sought to free themselves from the debased values of the 19th century was Dante Gabriel Rossetti (1828–82), a founder member of that group of painters which styled itself the 'Pre-Raphaelite Brotherhood' in 1848. With his fellow members of the PRB he came to believe in the mediaeval period as a sort of 'golden age' in which the arts were truly valued, in which honesty in craftsmanship flourished and in which religion, romantic love and chivalry still held their place and man was in harmony with nature. William Morris to some degree embraced these ideas too, though perhaps he was more concerned with a reorganisation of society on socialist lines rather than immersing himself in a new found romanticism. The cabinet by William Burges which houses a three-train, quarter striking clock was in tune with the ideas of Rossetti and Morris, and in it we find a parody of French Gothic art, with high-pitched roof, a machicolated parapet hung with bells, pointed arches and crowning pinnacles and Gothic lettering of uncial form. William Burges was an individualist and this extraordinary essay in Gothic design, ponderously heavy and expensively made about 1875 for a private client, cannot be held as typical of its day. It should only be judged as an eccentric expression of Gothic design in a piece of furniture which housed a clock, as desks and cabinets made in France in the 18th century had previously done. It expressed an idea which represented a challenge to those who used Gothic as a medium of design in a more mundane and commercial way, and before the designers and architects of the early 20th century were to sweep the style entirely away.

The architectural and decorative style in France corresponding to the Victorian revivals in England is known as 'Louis-Philippe and Napoleon III'. Louis-Philippe came to the Bourbon monarchy, which had been restored after Waterloo, in 1830, and in 1848 he was overthrown as the last king of France, to be replaced by Napoleon III, Emperor of the second Republic. Napoleon III met his defeat in the Franco-Prussian war of 1870 which marked the beginning of the third Republic. It was in the early years of this epoch, in the 1830s, that a passion for Gothic design influenced French furniture, the time when the archaeologist J-B-A Lassus (1807–57) was conducting his researches on Chartres Cathedral, and who later collaborated with E. E. Violet-le-Duc (1814–79) and began to rebuild, in the name of restoration, parts of major French Gothic cathedrals such as Notre Dame in Paris. By the 1850s French taste had re-embraced the Renaissance manner, which it had never entirely lost, and this is the principal style used in French clocks of the 19th century.

French skills in the handling of cast and chased bronze, which created such superlative work in the 18th century and Empire period, produced a number of clocks in the Gothic style in the 1830s, romantic assemblies of Gothic structure and decorative details known as 'à la cathédrale'. Only occasionally did the Gothic style show itself again in French 19th-century clocks, and even then in a form which is but a pale reflection of Gothic, reminiscent more of the 16th-century style of Early Renaissance châteaux. Such a clock is a mantel version in gilded bronze and alabaster, from the Paris house of Henri Marc, recorded in

Opposite page
French mantel clock in alabaster with gilded mounts; its style is reminiscent of early French Renaissance châteaux, with elements of Gothic, but not really Gothic in form; movement signed Henri Marc, Paris; about 1870. *Stuart Hall Collection*

the Avenue d'Eylau in 1870. In style it is Gothic/Early Renaissance, surmounted by a cupola which houses a bell, with Gothic 'black letter' numerals in gold on the alabaster dial, and cusped pediment with figures of soldiers in mediaeval chain-mail, guarding the sides above trophies of arms. Perhaps this design should be called 'château-esque' for it has little resemblance to pure Gothic of the Middle Ages, or indeed to Burges's Gothic desk with a clock, made in England about the same time.

With Gothic revival styles of the 19th century we have come, as it were, full circle from the beginning of this book, when Gothic architectural forms influenced the styles of frames of the first mechanical domestic clocks made in Europe. John Ruskin (1819–1900), who had decided views about the use of Gothic as a decorative style, was one of the most important art critics and arbiters of taste in his day, and held the Slade Professorship of Art at Oxford from 1869 to 1879. His huge series of lectures, pamphlets and books on the arts included *The Seven Lamps of Architecture* which was published in 1849, and it illustrates well the Christian criteria by which he judged art and architecture. In the last section of the book, 'The Lamp of Obedience', he discussed the choice of style on which designs should be based, allowing for individuality of expression, for '*modern uses in general*' in the following way:

'I cannot conceive any architect insane enough to project the vulgarisation of Greek architecture. Neither can it be rationally questionable whether we should adopt early or late, original or derivative Gothic; if the latter were chosen, it must be either some impotent and ugly degradation, like our own Tudor, or else a style whose grammatical laws it would be nearly impossible to limit or arrange, like the French Flamboyant. We are equally precluded from adopting styles essentially infantine or barbarous, however Herculean their infancy, or majestic their outlawry, such as our own Norman, or the Lombard Romanesque. The choice would lie I think between four styles: 1 The Pisan Romanesque; 2 The early Gothic of the Western Italian Republics, advanced as far and as fast as our art would enable us to the Gothic of Giotto; 3 The Venetian Gothic in its purest development; 4 The English earliest decorated. The most natural, perhaps the safest choice, would be of the last, well fenced from chance of again stiffening into the perpendicular; and perhaps enriched by some mingling of decorative elements from the exquisite decorated Gothic of France, of which, in such cases, it would be needful to accept some well-known examples, as the North door of Rouen and the church of St. Urbain at Troyes, for final and limiting authorities on the side of decoration.'

ART AND INDUSTRY: II
Renaissance Revivals and Art Nouveau

Although the Gothic revival style in the 19th century had a significant vogue in England and America, the predominant style from about the beginning of Queen Victoria's reign in 1837 to the outbreak of the First World War, was classical or Renaissance revival, particularly in the later decades. To try to simplify the situation by grouping everything under the general heading of 'Renaissance' would be misleading in the extreme, for what is really meant is that a multiplicity of styles was used, such as Early Renaissance—Elizabethan and Jacobean; High Renaissance—Palladian and Baroque; 18th century Renaissance—Rococo and Neo-Classical; and various interpretations of these as found in England, America, Germany and France, and often of so bewildering a mixture of styles as to defy description. Such an example is a pottery-cased clock of the last quarter of the 19th century, an astonishing 'tour de force' of applied ornament justifying Dr Nikolaus Pevsner's remarks in *High Victorian Design* (1951) that 'An age which frankly applied art to objects instead of thinking in terms of aesthetic value from the beginning of the designing process, could hardly find fault more readily with the Elizabethan piano than with the Egyptian steam engine or the Gothic railway station'.

The ceramic clock illustrated on the book jacket is nearly 2 ft (61 cm) high and is made of cream-coloured earthenware, coloured under the glaze and gilded here and there on its surface. Most of its decorative features owe their origin to Baroque, but of a style which would have horrified Wren and his architectural contemporaries. Surmounted by a vase with dolphin caryatids, the segmental pediment has two winged cherubs and flanking corner vases balanced by Greek acroteria at the rear, and pendants below the architrave. Below the dial a satyr's head grins out from under a veritable cornucopia of coloured fruits, while at each corner full-breasted winged sphinxes with lions' paws support the whole of this phantasmagoric composition. The side panels are ornamented in relief with flaming altars and other Roman ornament, and not content with this riot of design the French retailer, H. Houderine of the Rue Torenne in Paris, applied a porcelain dial with Roman numerals in white reserves on blue, the centre decorated with Venus and Cupid on a ground of gold. A clock of this type, originally protected from dust and damage by a tall glass shade, might almost be called surrealistic in its incongruous grouping of architectural and historical forms. The clock's very existence indicates a confusion of thought and incongruity of associated elements which is reflected in the design of many domestic objects of the 19th century, and in certain cases which persists today.

Far more pleasing in its refined, glazed white porcelain case is the example from the Minton Museum, Stoke-on-Trent, made about 1875. On the base of the case, clearly seen at the front, there is a firing crack which probably prevented this piece from being sold by the Minton Company, consequently it remains without a movement today. The movement intended would have been a standard French drum type.

Mantel clock case in glazed bone china; a slight firing crack prevented this clock from being completed and sold; French movement intended but not fitted; made by Mintons, Stoke-on-Trent; about 1875. *Minton Museum, Royal Doulton Tableware Ltd*

Mantel clock with quarter-striking
Westminster chimes; mahogany case
with gilded bronze mounts; attributed to
F. W. Elliott, London, but not signed;
about 1890. *Stuart Hall Collection*

Venus and Cupid, with the pair of doves, continue a Renaissance theme
which was popular, especially in French clocks. This example, of which
the designer/modeller is not recorded, is in keeping with Mintons'
output in other types of pottery and porcelain when Renaissance revival
styles were very much the fashion. It is likely that this porcelain case was
intended to be gilded and enamelled in colours, but its elegance and
charm are not diminished by its present unfinished and slightly dam-
aged state.

The ready availability of small French movements produced a vast
range of cases in England into which they could be fitted, but the
heavier and more cumbersome English movements generally required
larger and heavier cases to house them. To illustrate two examples from
the later years of the 19th century shows how a good quality traditional
'Renaissance' style of clock could be made while new ideas were appearing, also inspired by the past, but in a completely different way.

The first clock is an enormously heavy three-train, quarter-striking (Westminster chimes) eight-day mantel version in a mahogany case, with gilded bronze mounts. It has been attributed to the firm of F. W. Elliott Limited of London who undoubtedly made such types, but in its unsigned state it could have been made by other London firms such as Barraud & Lund. Such clocks as this were popular both in the board-room and the domestic parlour until well into the 20th century. At first glance the style of the case is positively 18th century, with pineapple finials on the 'true bell' top, herms at the corners, bracket feet and pierced side frets. Two or three features stand out strongly to show that the clock is not 18th century (without looking at the movement), and these concern the dial. Although the silvered chapter ring is mounted on a matted brass dial-plate, with subsidiary dials at the top, 18th-century clocks of break-arch form were not shaped as a semi-circular arch integral with the vertical sides; nor, generally, were their glazed fronts fitted with a heavy moulded metal bezel, at least until the later years of the Georgian era, for this feature is nearer to French than English taste. A further feature proclaims this design as a 19th-century version of 18th-century style, this being the silvered 'sight plate' as it is sometimes called, screwed to the inside of the wooden door frame and provided to hide the gap between the glass and the dial itself. No case of this kind could possibly deceive the observer as to its date, but sometimes it is not easy to be instantly certain as to whether or not it is English or German, for many clocks were made in a similar style for the English market by German manufacturers.

The second English clock with a heavy two-train movement comes from a ceramic manufacturer, and not a clock made in quantity for the general market, but a 'one-off' in the studio tradition, an off-shoot from the Arts and Crafts movement outlined in the previous chapter. This is the product of a gifted artist employed by Messrs Mintons of Stoke-

Below left
Clock probably originally part of a cabinet or desk; ebonised wooden case with alabaster rings on the columns; fitted with pâte-sur-pâte porcelain panels by M. L. Solon; clock movement signed John Mortlock and Co., London; about 1885. *Minton Museum, Royal Doulton Tableware Ltd*

Below right
Mantel clock in salt-glazed stoneware case; designed by Eliza Simmance and made by Doultons of Lambeth; French movement; 1890–95

on-Trent. Mintons were far-sighted in their design policy, engaging talented artists such as Léon Arnoux who came to Herbert Minton's factory as Art Director in 1849, and another Frenchman who had worked at the Sèvres porcelain factory, Marc-Louis Solon (d 1913). Solon, who made the plaques for the case of this English clock, joined Mintons during the Franco–Prussian war in 1870, and was responsible for the introduction of the ceramic art of pâte-sur-pâte for which the firm became justly famous, and this is the material from which the plaques in the clock are made. The clock case has eleven plaques set into an ebonised and gilded wooden frame, with alabaster rings on the corner columns. From its general appearance and certain structural details it would seem that this clock originally formed part of a larger scheme for a cabinet or desk, of which the rest is missing. Furniture incorporating ceramic plaques or tiles had become relatively common in the 1890s when this clock was made.

Pâte-sur-pâte is a ceramic technique in which a semi-liquid parian porcelain clay is painted, laboriously, in successive layers, to build up images of figures or ornament on a dark coloured porcelain ground, and when the finished work is fired and glazed the applied decoration becomes semi-translucent, delicate and subtle. Solon was a master of this art and his source of inspiration in his vases and plaques, as in this clock case, was the Renaissance style in several forms, as from the paintings of the Rococo artists Boucher and Fragonard or from the Neo-Classicism of Ingres or Flaxman. As in French clocks of Louis XVI, Solon simply regarded the case as an opportunity to employ his art, though his designs are not entirely unrelated to the clock itself for there is allegorical symbolism in the cupids disporting themselves round the globe of the Earth, in the flanking female figures in Neo-Classical pose, with scythes in their hands, and in the head of Diana above, with a crescent moon. It is a pity that Solon took no part in designing the dial, for the one which was fitted would have been far more suitable in a Gothic case, since its numerals contain traces of Celtic

Skeleton clock with scrolled brass frame; probably made by James Edwards of Stourbridge; signed W. Mayo, Manchester; 1830–40

Right
Skeleton clock with scrolled brass frame and unusual movement utilising epicyclic gearing; designed by William Strutt and made by William Wigston, Derby; 1820–30

art and its hands are uncompromisingly of Gothic trefoil design. The clock movement was supplied by the firm of John Mortlock & Co. as a necessary complement to the far more important artistic design of the complete cabinet, and not of particular importance in itself.

Another famous English pottery manufactory, which occasionally made clock cases, was the Thames-side pottery of Doultons in Lambeth. Although makers of 'useful' wares, the Doulton company began a revival of 'Art' pottery at Lambeth in 1866 in association with Mr John Sparkes and his students at the Lambeth School of Art. Their decorative pottery was made in a ceramic fabric called salt-glazed stoneware in which, with the use of inspired modelling and the addition of coloured lead glazes, articles of great beauty and physical strength could be made. Several designs of clock cases, arranged to house standard French and German movements, were produced, the one illustrated being designed by a lady artist, Eliza Simmance in the early 1890s. It is hardly necessary to comment on the classical architectural structure of this clock case, and perhaps only relevant to add that forms such as this could be reproduced in quantity from plaster moulds. Other pottery firms, mostly in north Staffordshire, made cheap and sometimes tawdry ceramic clock cases with crude decoration to house mostly German movements, and there were many cheaply made Continental cases too.

Ceramic clock cases were never as popular in 19th-century France as in England, for the traditional French metal-cased trade remained firmly established. However, a porcelain clock from one of the Parisian

Above left
French mantel clock in a case of gilded and enamelled Paris porcelain; the style is pure Rococo revival; standard French drum movement signed Thomas à Paris; about 1850. *The Bowes Museum, Barnard Castle, Co. Durham*

Above right
French mantel clock in a gilded bronze case of Baroque inspiration; dial and four panels of blue and white enamel; maker of case and movement unknown; about 1870. *Stuart Hall Collection*

factories, of richly enamelled and gilded Rococo design, reminds us of the adherence of French 19th-century designers to classical revival forms. One might be forgiven for expecting this clock to be 18th century at first glance, but the 'C' scrolls are heavy and the modelling of the romantic couple at the top of the clock shows clearly the 19th-century treatment of their heads, like a Parisian dress-designer's fashion-plate. Rococo scrollwork in English 19th-century clocks appears more usually in skeleton clock frames than in other types of case, and in modified form the classical tradition in the skeleton clock should be compared with the Gothic type seen in the previous chapter.

In keeping with the spirit of the Renaissance, English skeleton clocks with scrolled frames have open curves which give a clearer view of the working parts than Gothic skeletons, and two are shown of this design. The first is a clock of great simplicity, possibly from the firm of James Edwards of Stourbridge in Worcestershire. The name of the retailer on the dial is William Mayo of Manchester who was in business in the 1830s and '40s, but the chances that Mayo made this piece are slim indeed. The late Mr F. B. Royer-Collard identified many of the actual manufacturers of English skeleton clocks including W. F. Evans of the Soho Factory at Handsworth in Birmingham whose Scott Memorial clock has been illustrated. Others were James Edwards of Stourbridge, a number of makers in the Liverpool area, John Smith & Sons of St John's Square, Clerkenwell in London and the Haycock Brothers at Ashbourne in Derbyshire. So widespread was the range of styles and number of skeleton clocks produced that doubtless many others were engaged in the trade. One such was William Strutt (1756–1830) who invented a curious type of skeleton clock with epicyclic gearing which was made in the 1820s at the Derby factory of Strutt's friend William Wigston, who was a manufacturer of rotary machines. The 'sun and planet' type of gearing which the clock employs provided a fascinating visual point of interest, and the principle was well known to the engineers who designed steam engines at that time. As an engineer himself Wigston, no doubt assisted by Strutt, made the original production of about 20 examples with sun and planet gears. Strutt's design was revived in the 1850s and made in larger numbers in a modified form, but in these later examples by a London firm no name of the real manufacturer was given. Originality, mechanical ingenuity and visual accessibility are the keynote of these once neglected Victorian clocks.

To return to French clocks of the 19th century, the volume of Renaissance revivals is vast, and only a few can be shown from a range of infinite possibilities. All are classical in style, the first being of Baroque architectural design in which the circular drum movement is 'suspended', as it were, from the sides and top of the clock in a manner vaguely reminiscent of the Empire style. The central vase above the broken pediment has reliefs of Apollo (day) and Diana (night), while the centre dial, numerals, tympana panels and two panels on the base are in white enamel on a rich blue ground. No name on either dial or movement is found on this clock, but another in the Rococo manner and of somewhat earlier date, is signed André à Paris, from the Rue de Chaillot about 1850, the movement being by Schuller who is recorded at the Rue Transnonain in the 1830s and '40s. The floral enamelled porcelain panel below the dial is the central attractive feature of this clock, in a gilded Rococo-inspired case, but of heavier style than true Rococo. Yet another 19th-century French mantel clock in this genre is a completely metal-cased version surmounted by rural lovers, in the manner of Boucher, in a floral bocage, but exposing its real origin in the modelling of the figures which have a 19th and not an 18th-century flavour.

Perhaps most typical of all 19th-century French clocks is a garniture set supplied to that indomitable collector of French art, John Bowes, in 1854. Its porcelain vases are mounted in ormolu stands of most opulent form, supported by winged cupids, the central vase above the clock itself being richly enamelled with a scene of Venus and her attendants, rising from the waves (see p. 135). The essential architectural and decorative ingredients in this set are Neo-Classical, but so heavily and profusely are they organised that the whole composition does not even resemble the delicate and cool quality of true Neo-Classical design.

Eclecticism utilising a variety of Renaissance sources was not confined, in the 19th century, to English and French clock case design, for there continued to be an inter-relationship of European forms with popular American styles throughout the century, and especially from the 1870s onwards. We have already seen how the American makers had been influenced by European tradition in the first half of the century and as competition between the expanding German and Black Forest industries and America increased, so American manufacturers found it necessary to emulate European styles ever more closely.

To illustrate the way in which American clockmaking factories competed with their English rivals, several 19th-century clock design styles have been chosen to illustrate how American manufacturers brought out similar styles, frequently making use of imitative materials and at a considerably lower price. It is not always easy to be certain whether the Americans copied the Germans, or the other way round. In the case of the Vienna regulator there would seem little doubt that this extremely popular type of wall clock, with its carved wooden eagle, its heavily turned ebony or ebonised columns, its turned and half-split ornaments

Above left
French mantel clock in Rococo revival case of gilded bronze with a floral porcelain panel at the front; movement signed Schuller à Paris; dial signed André à Paris; about 1850. *Stuart Hall Collection*

Above right
French mantel clock in a completely gilded bronze case crowned by a Boucher-style pair of rural lovers; movement signed Taveau Frères à Paris; maker of case unknown; 1850–60. *Stuart Hall Collection*

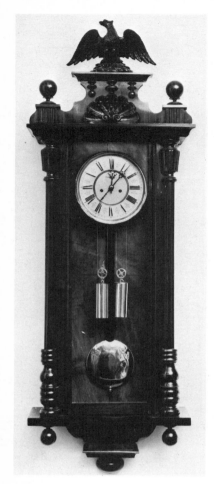

BAGDAD. Dial, 8 inches.   CAPITOL. Dial, 8 inches.   PROMPT. Dial, 8 inches.

MALTA.

ENAMELED IRON.

8 Day, Half-hour Strike, Gong.
STAR MOVEMENT.
Height 10¼ inches.   Length 19¼ inches.
Dial 5½ inches, Porcelain or Fine Gilt.
With or Without Visible Escapement.

Above left
Wall-hanging clock popularly known as a
Vienna regulator; veneered walnut with
ebony columns and other ornament;
maker unknown; about 1890. *Stuart Hall
Collection*

Above right
Page 51 from the Catalogue of the
Ansonia Clock Company, New York,
illustrating three American 'Vienna'
regulators; 1880

Centre right
French mantel clock; case of black
polished slate or marble; bronze reliefs
and columns; unsigned, but presentation
plate dated 1900

Below right
Page 47 from the Catalogue of the
Waterbury Clock Company illustrating an
American enamelled iron clock in the
style of European black slate-cased
mantel clocks; 1891

and its glass front, was the source of inspiration for a range of clocks published in the catalogue of the Ansonia Clock Company of New York, issued in 1880. In a similar way the Connecticut factory of the Waterbury Clock Company in its catalogue of 1891 advertised black mantel clocks, sometimes known in America as 'blacks' or 'marblized clocks' to compete with a wide range of Continental black slate or marble clocks, mostly with French movements fitted into Belgian slate cases. As a cheaper version of the same idea the American clock was of enamelled cast-iron, but similarly ornamented with a colonnade of columns in the classical manner. Even the visible escapement on the dial of this American clock was a copy of an idea which started on fine quality clocks in France in the late 18th century.

The story of the debt which American designers owed to Europe in producing an elaborate profusion of clock case designs in the late 19th century has still to be written, but one type of particular interest is the Anglo-American clock. The trunk dial clock mentioned in the seventh chapter had become a most popular clock in England for schools, offices, banks etc. and frequently used in the domestic kitchen. Its secure position, hanging on a wall, and its generally good quality of movement, made it a reliable and worthy timepiece, and in style it was copied under the American name of a drop-dial. An English eight-day trunk dial of high quality in a mahogany case inlaid with mother-of-pearl is illustrated alongside another version which came on the market at about the same date, probably in the 1870s. The second clock has an American movement by the Ansonia Clock Company, but it is in an English case. Little is yet known about this type of Anglo-American co-operative venture which produced two basic types of case, the drop-dial noted and another version with flanking columns and a mirror behind the pendulum, seen through the glazed trunk door. Various minor variations of these two basic Anglo-American designs are known, but all are characterised by a decorative form of patterned veneering done in the manner of Tunbridge ware. That type of geometric veneering developed early at Tunbridge Wells in Kent and in the 19th century became extremely popular for ornamental boxes, trays and small pieces of furniture. This veneer is not an inlay, but was put together in a continuous strip and applied to the cases in diverse ways. Mr E. J. Tyler has isolated one firm which imported American movements to be housed in cases such as these, the London establishment of Holloway & Co., and has also suggested that Italian labour may have been used for this craft. Until examples are found with identifying labels, or until American records are discovered, naming customers in England to whom movements only were retailed, it is not possible to discuss their origin further, but that these cases are not American has been confirmed by many authorities in the United States, nor do these designs appear in American clock catalogues.

A type of clock which first appeared in the American Ansonia 1880 catalogue is known as a 'swinger'. It was well known in Germany, with certain more sophisticated versions in France. In this type of clock the movement and dial form the upper part of a long compound pendulum, for which a smaller not visible pendulum on the movement proper provides the impulse, supported on the outstretched arm of a figure, or sometimes on the trunk of a miniature elephant or other support. The Junghans factory in Germany made clocks of this kind and a splendid example of a French sculptured bronze figure supporting such a clock takes this chapter to the introduction of an artistic style known as Art Nouveau. In typical French manner the appeal of this clock is in its draped female figure, of elegant pose, poetically entitled 'Brise

English wall-hanging clock known as a trunk dial; mahogany case with mother of pearl inlays; maker unknown; about 1875. *Stuart Hall Collection*

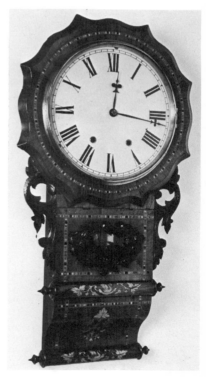

Wall-hanging clock in a marquetry veneered case of English make; fitted with an American movement by the Ansonia Clock Company, New York; this type of clock known as Anglo-American; about 1875. *Stuart Hall Collection*

French figure clock in bronze with suspended clock as part of the pendulum; the figure sculpture is called *Brise d'Automne* by Auguste Moreau; about 1900. *Stuart Hall Collection*

d'Automne' and modelled by the Parisian sculptor Auguste Moreau who exhibited at the Paris Salon in 1861 and practised his art until 1910. The flowing, restless lines of this exotic figure express a spirit which is not simply a new version of a classical idea. To some extent like the figures on Solon's Minton clock case she typifies a new breath of air which was to sweep through Europe and was to drive away that dependence on Gothic or classical ideas which were the overwhelming influence of the 19th century in art, architecture and design.

Art Nouveau and the Aesthetic Movement followed in the path of the Arts and Crafts Movement which started with William Morris in the 1860s. Many influences contributed to this style, but one which was to have its effect in the second half of the 19th century, before the name Art Nouveau was ever thought of, was the Japanese style. From the early years of the 17th century, when the Dutch and Portuguese had taken European clocks to that far-off country, Japan's doors had been closed to western culture until international treaties were finally negotiated in 1854. It was the desire for an aesthetic renewal in the world of the arts that certain painters, sculptors, designers and some architects seized on Japanese ideas as a fresh and vital breeze, to fill the west with strange new qualities and standards of taste. The painter James Abbott McNeill Whistler (1834–1903), born an American but who spent most of his life in London and Paris, was influenced through an almost accidental contact with Japanese wood-block prints from the hand of the artist Hokusai and others, which had come into Europe as packing materials. A shop for selling oriental objects of art was opened in 1862 in the Rue de Rivoli in Paris which attracted another influential painter, Henry Fantin-Latour (1836–1904), and many of the French Impressionist and Post-Impressionist painters also came under the influence of Japanese art, in which they saw a use of colour and composition of pictures in a way which was new, fresh and exciting. Rossetti in England, even in his dream-world of romantic mediaevalism, had his cabinet of Oriental porcelain. One of the great monuments of this enthusiasm for another dream-world of Oriental imagery is Whistler's *Peacock Room*, painted for his patron Frederick R. Leyland in his house at 49 Prince's Gate, London, in 1863–4, but now in the Freer Gallery in Washington. Here Whistler painted a fanciful array of gorgeous peacocks and flowers, on a ground of old Spanish leather, with his framed canvas *Rose and Silver: The Princess from the Land of Porcelain* on the end wall. That Leyland was far from pleased when he saw the result is of no account today, for this fabulous room with Whistler's paintings remains as a monument to what came to be called the 'Aesthetic Movement' of the later 19th century.

The Aesthetic Movement with its interest in Japanese and other Oriental art did not go unnoticed by the furniture designers of that time, and two particularly, William Burges and his friend E. W. Godwin (1833–86) were to be influenced by the style. Later the influence of Japanese art affected the designs of clocks by C. R. Mackintosh and the Austrian Sezessionist school of Art Nouveau. In a more 'commercial' sense a French clock garniture set is noted, with its porcelain vases and clock case panels covered in Japanese-inspired designs of gilded birds, butterflies and flowers, curiously associated with Renaissance architectural features of Corinthian columns and vase-shaped finials. The maker of this case and matching vases is unknown, but in its design the cultures of east and west have come together in a strange intermingling.

The influence and ideas which created the Aesthetic Movement and Art Nouveau may partly be understood by looking at the work of a small pottery in the north-west of England, at Birkenhead, where a few

Right
Mantel clock in an earthenware case
designed by Ruth Bare and made at the
Della Robbia Pottery Company,
Birkenhead; English movement;
about 1902

Below left
Longcase clock in the Vienna Sezession
style with inlaid floral designs; influenced
by Japanese art especially in the
overhanging cornice and detached
square columns; Art Nouveau hands;
maker unknown; about 1910. *City Art
Gallery, Manchester*

Below right
Small bedside alarm clock with a
conventional spring-powered
movement; moulded plastic case;
luminous hands; card dial made in West
Germany; about 1980

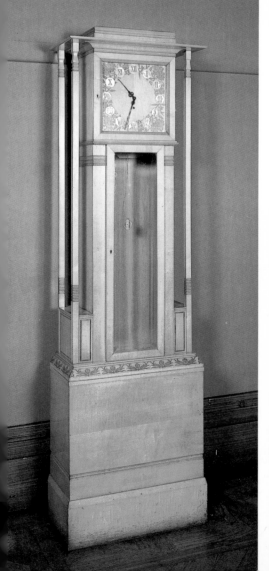

clock cases were made. These cases illustrate how artists, working in a small studio in the 1890s and early 1900s, could adapt past styles and yet bring to their work an individual and artistic quality as a reaction to the world of cheap and often ill-designed mass-production which lay all around them.

The Birkenhead Della Robbia Pottery Company was comparatively short-lived, lasting only from 1894 to 1906, under the inspired guidance of its proprietor Harold Rathbone. Rathbone founded it with 'the intention of restoring to the worker the individual interest and pleasure in daily work and creation'. This ideal of pleasure in craftsmanship was close to the feelings of William Morris and the Della Robbia studio allowed its employees to develop their individual talents in the ceramic media. Its inspiration came partly from the Florentine world of the Della Robbia family and its motifs were derived from Renaissance, and sometimes Islamic sources, though it also may be identified with the aspirations of the new style of Art Nouveau. A clock case modelled by Ruth Bare about 1902 is very much in the Art Nouveau manner, a composition of stems, leaves and flowers in flowing, inter-twined curves closely related to some metal-cased clocks to be seen later (see p. 136). The curves of the roots and stems on the front and sides of the case flow like Celtic interlaced zoomorphic forms of the 8th and 9th centuries, yet not so involved and rich. In the flower heads and leaves there are echoes of the Pre-Raphaelites, coupled with shaded greens and blues of the under-glaze colours. The whole composition is monumental and yet languorous, of an intensity of feeling and period flavour which, curiously enough, marries quite well with the German-style dial which has numerals like those on Solon's Mortlock clock behind which is an English movement. The Della Robbia Pottery was famous for its architectural ceramic panels, mouldings and decorative sculpture, and something of the quality of architectural dignity is to be felt in Ruth Bare's composition.

Art Nouveau, or 'New Art' is the name given to a decorative art style which spread through Europe and America in the 1890s. It had a major influence in the early years of the present century, its effects sometimes still to be found in furniture elaborated with tendrils and flowers and

Plate 33 from the Catalogue of the Ansonia Clock Company, New York, illustrating an American 'swinger'; 1880

French clock garniture set in polished brass with porcelain panels and vases decorated with Japanese-inspired enamelled designs; movement signed Mougin, Paris; case maker unknown; about 1890. *Stuart Hall Collection*

Mantel clock in a silver-plated, oxidised
and hammer-finished case with applied
cast reliefs; French movement;
A. Edward Jones Ltd, Birmingham;
about 1920

heart-shaped holes. The style was, in a sense, a direct development from
the Arts and Crafts Movement, followed by the Aesthetic Movement,
and it began in the architectural field with the designs of the Belgian
architect Victor Horta (1861–1947) who decorated the interior of his
house at No. 12 Rue de Turin in Brussels in 1893 in a series of swirling
writhing curves of ironwork and mosaics. There were many craftsmen
and designers at this time such as Arthur H. Mackmurdo (1851–1942)
who founded the Century Guild in 1882, and C. R. Ashbee (1863–1942)
who founded the Guild and School of Handicraft in 1888. While accepting Morris's concept of the virtues of hand craftsmanship, they rejected
the dependence on styles of the past and strove to find their way
towards a new, non-historical mode of expression, at the same time not
accepting the products of the machine. With astonishing swiftness the
new style manifested itself in painting, sculpture, print-making and
decorative design for about ten years between 1895 and 1905, known as
the Jugendstil in Germany, derived from the name of the journal *Jugend*
(Youth) which was published in 1896. The name 'Art Nouveau' was
generally adopted when the art dealer and historian Samuel Bing
(1838–1905) first opened his shop at No. 22 Rue de Provence in Paris in
1895, and put in front of the fashionable world the works of such
progressive craftsmen as the American glass-maker Louis Comfort
Tiffany (1848–1933) or silverware and jewellery from the New York
firm of Tiffany & Co.

Other artists and designers who had a part to play in the Art Nouveau
movement included the illustrator Aubrey Beardsley (1872–98) whose
drawings for Oscar Wilde's *Salome* so shocked the world in the era
known as the 'fin de siècle', C. F. A. Voysey, C. R. Mackintosh whose
clock cases we shall see later, the painter and poster artist Alphonse
Mucha (1860–1939), and the creator of the first work of graphic art in
the Art Nouveau manner, A. H. Mackmurdo.

Like most new vogues or styles which originally came from the
imagination of creative artists, it was not long before the commercial

world sought to exploit Art Nouveau for profit and gain, although in fairness it must be said that commercial outlets gave a living to practising craftsmen. One of the leading London firms which offered commissions to craftsmen in the late 19th century was Liberty & Co., founded in 1875 in the Strand. The name of Liberty became so well known for the promotion of objects in the Art Nouveau style that in Italy the movement was called the Stile Liberty. The founder of the company, Arthur Lasenby Liberty, first took the firm into the silversmithing trade in 1894. In 1901, in association with the Birmingham firm of W. H. Haseler, a new company known as Liberty & Co. (Cymric) Ltd was registered. A 'Cymric' clock design in silver from the early years of the present century shows the Art Nouveau mannerisms of swelling sides, convoluted front and flowing, scrolled foliage, but the more recent design of the hands of the clock perhaps suggests a later date of actual production, or later replacement. A designer who is recorded as having worked for Liberty was Archibald Knox (1864–1933) from the Isle of Man, and a clock case in beaten copper is illustrated which is attributed to him. In this example the hands are certainly original, and its handhammered repoussé numerals are typical of the attempts by designers at that time to produce lettering in a modern 'hand-crafted' form, more in keeping with a hand-made case than formal Roman or Arabic numerals would have been.

From about 1902 a Birmingham silversmith, Albert Edward Jones (1878–1954) established a small workshop employing only a handful of craftsmen to produce silver and bronze bowls, candlesticks, tea sets, clocks, trays, condiment sets and other small domestic objects of this type, in considerable quantity. Jones had been much influenced by his association with many of the leading craftsmen of his day, and in 1933 he took over the firm of Hardman Powells of Birmingham which had been responsible for much ecclesiastical metalwork, inspired by Pugin. Although the First World War caused the firm to turn to constructing aluminium parts for military aeroplanes, after the war Jones made a wide range of silver-plated, oxidised and hammer-finished clocks using standard French movements. Strictly speaking this clock of about 1920 does not belong to the Arts and Crafts movement, nor to the vogue for Art Nouveau, but it is in the tradition of the early years of the 20th century, with its hand-hammered case, its applied cast leaf and flower bosses round the dial, and its extraordinary elongated and tapered legs swelling to pad-like feet. Jones had used this feature in his designs for vases about 1905, and it may be related to the overall form of the ceramic clock case by Ruth Bare of the Della Robbia Pottery.

One of the most interesting features of the work of late 19th and early 20th-century designers of clocks—that is of quality clocks for an exclusive market and not the mass-produced products of the factory system—is the way in which they sought to retain high standards of hand-craftsmanship, keeping some elements of traditional clock case design, yet investing the final product with a 'modern' aspect. An example of this is a mantel clock by Charles Francis Annesley Voysey (1857–1941) of 1906. Voysey was one of the most important and influential furniture designers and architects of his day, who identified himself closely with the Arts and Crafts movement, becoming a member of the *Art Workers' Guild* in 1884 and its Master 40 years later. Although a designer of furniture, metalwork, wallpapers, textiles, tiles and carpets, Voysey was also an architect best known for a handful of country houses totally designed, down to the last detail, by himself, though his ordinary country house commissions had otherwise extended widely from the early 1890s. Although primarily a designer,

Mantel clock in oak designed by C. F. A. Voysey; Continental striking movement; 1906. *The Geffrye Museum, London*

and not a craftsman, the characteristic feature we see in his work is his total commitment to vernacular design, extending English traditional qualities and character into his newly-evolved schemes. Thus the mantel clock he designed is of plain, unvarnished ebony and oak, its pegged joints showing as in 17th century oak furniture, its 'belfry' or pagoda top retaining echoes of 18th century Oriental taste, its ball feet and finial also characteristic of 17th-century design, with classical mouldings on the plinth and cornice. Yet all this adds up to a style which is of the early 20th century, with well-designed Arabic numerals of calligraphic form, reminding us of the revival of interest in letter forms and penmanship by the great English contemporary calligrapher Edward Johnston. The hands of the clock retain the contrast of shape between the hour and the minute hands which was so typical of late 17th-century styles, and incorporate the heart-shaped 'spade' which was a decorative detail commonly used by Voysey.

A contemporary of C. F. A. Voysey who was faced with the same problems, but solved them differently, was the Scottish designer Charles Rennie Mackintosh (1868–1928), whose solutions to the problems of designing clock cases had little, if any, effect on the popular market for clocks, but whose powers were to influence later ideas in the 20th century, and to release that dependence on 19th-century revivalism. Mackintosh was born in Glasgow where he practised as an architect and furniture designer for most of his life, apart from a few years in Chelsea and his last five years when he lived in France. The great architect Mies van der Rohe described Mackintosh's work as being 'a purifier' and talked about his ideas for the School of Art in Glasgow as being 'the beginning of a breakthrough'. That 'breakthrough' was Mackintosh's extraordinary vision, his creation of new ideas, new motifs, brand new concepts in decoration and proportion. Underneath his style one can detect a basic training in classical ideas of proportion and balance, but his genius modelled the precepts of classicism and the honesty of Scottish vernacular design, into something which was wholly 'modern' and which still seems so today, in the 1980s. Mackintosh's work was received with enthusiasm on the Continent where he became well known as the Art Nouveau exponent of the Glasgow School. Charles Rennie Mackintosh is probably best remembered for his designs for the Glasgow School of Art in 1896, and for the decoration and furniture for Miss Cranston's Buchanan and Argyle Street tea-rooms in Glasgow in 1897. He is certainly remembered for his enormously elongated chairs which were hardly for sitting upon, but had a marvellous 'presence' and monumental character wherever they were placed. After many architectural commissions he virtually gave up designing buildings during the First World War, concentrating rather on furniture and textiles, and finally turning to painting landscape watercolours.

During the later years of the First World War Mackintosh produced a series of mantel clock designs which, looking back at them about 65 years later, are remarkable in showing how he struggled with the problem of 'modernising' the traditional clock dial, quite apart from the unconventional nature of his solution to the complete case form. A Mackintosh clock at the Hunterian Museum in Glasgow of about 1915 shows a dial in ebony and inlaid ivory with a conventional grouping of Roman numerals and spade-type hands, but by 1919 we can see from a series of drawings how he attempted to bring the detailing of the dials of his clocks into new realms of conception. An intriguing solution was the 'domino' idea in which each numeral, shaped as an isosceles triangular plaque creating a 'star' effect on the complete dial, was identified by

Mantel clock in ebonised wood with ivory inlays on the dial; standard French drum movement; designed by C. R. Mackintosh; about 1915. *Hunterian Art Gallery, University of Glasgow, Mackintosh Collection*

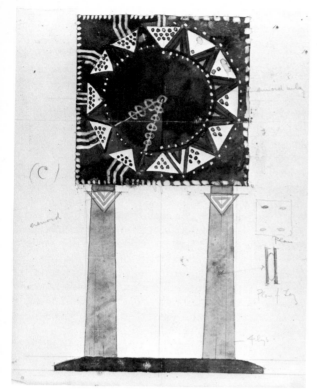

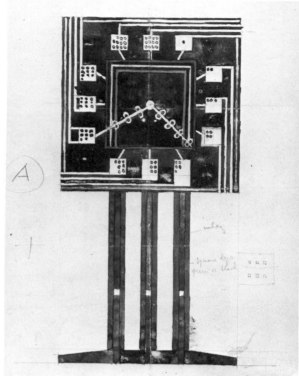

the relevant number of black dots or spots, to show the number of the hours. The increasing number of spots, from one to twelve, with their increasing effect of mass, creates a clockwise rhythm, and Mackintosh expanded on this idea in another layout where the numerals are rectangular plaques, arranged round a square dial, with horizontal and vertical lines emphasising clockwise movement. In these designs we might detect certain elements of Art Deco, which had arrived by the time of Mackintosh's death, in which geometrical forms provided the basis for a new approach to surface decoration. Like Voysey at the same time, Charles Rennie Mackintosh was finding new solutions to age-old traditional forms.

A final clock in the Art Nouveau style is a case which belongs to that group of artists/designers known as the Sezessionist School of Vienna (see p. 136), where Mackintosh's work was later highly regarded. Founded in the early 1890s, the group was brought together by the architect Josef Maria Olbrich (1867–1908) and the artist Gustave Klimt and others. In its early days the movement followed the flowing, twisting, whiplash style of Art Nouveau, but later, about 1898, it was influenced by Mackintosh and took on a more rigid architectural character, embracing those qualities of tradition and handcraftsmanship of the Arts and Crafts movement. The Vienna Sezession clock of about 1910 carries no name, but its structure and details inescapably link it to that school of design. The crisp, classically formed mouldings and stencil-like inlays are reminiscent of Voysey; the bevel-edged glass of the hood and trunk doors are pure Edwardian of popular furnishing style; the vertical Roman numerals in blue circular plaques raise memories of French dials, but in a vastly different spirit, and the four square detached columns with strong horizontal overhanging cornice remind us of Mackintosh's debt to Japanese design, which had been an important influence at the time of the Aesthetic Movement, and of the

Above left
Design for a clock in pencil and watercolour by C. R. Mackintosh; this design utilises the idea of dots for the numerals in triangular plaques; about 1919. *Hunterian Art Gallery, University of Glasgow, Mackintosh Collection*

Above right
Design for a clock in pencil and watercolour by C. R. Mackintosh; this design uses the dots for numerals but also expresses clockwise movement; about 1919. *Hunterian Art Gallery, University of Glasgow, Mackintosh Collection*

furniture of E. W. Godwin. Nowhere more traditional in this clock is the overall proportion of the case, and nowhere more indicative of its period and source is the flowing pattern of its elegant hands. It is a rare and superlative piece by any standards, and it is worth our while to compare it with a traditional clock of longcase form, made at roughly the same time for the ordinary 'establishment' market (see below).

Of all the clocks discussed in this section on Art Nouveau, none were made for the popular or ordinary commercial market. Most were the individual expressions of designers looking for a new approach to the design of traditional objects of furniture, largely at variance with a machine-made tradition, and even those produced for Liberty or by Jones of Birmingham being available only to a more or less exclusive clientèle. The efforts of progressive designers during the closing decades of the 19th century and the early years of the 20th, were eventually to help in concentrating the attention of an increasing number of people to the need for better design, and for an increased awareness of the shortcomings of the standards of taste in the western world at that time. The clocks shown here, therefore, are not intended to illustrate what was most fashionable during the years before and after 1900, but rather to show how the avant-garde were beginning to make their influence felt, just as the finest designers of all periods first made their ideas felt amongst the wealthy and the discerning, rather than in the ordinary market place. The architect and designer William Richard Lethaby (1857–1931) summed up the position perfectly in his essay from *Form in Civilisation: Collected Papers on Art and Labour*, first published in 1922, in which he wrote:

'We think in words, and we talk of architecture and fine design and art and style and so on, but we do not seem to notice with our eyes how little of these things we get in the real streets of the real towns we know—London and Leeds, Manchester and Macclesfield, Birmingham and Bristol. It is the real towns as they are that I want to get people to see, really to see with their eyes, not as statistics or as history, or as town planning on paper, as theory or style, but with their eyes, as they are . . . . If we agree in thinking that we should at least aim at bettering all these things, I want to suggest that we need a bigger centre and substance to work from than the personal one; we need a sense of citizenship, of public order, of national spirit.'

Lethaby was voicing 60 years ago a problem which is still with us today, the gulf which separates the dead historicism of much mass-produced design, and the sensitive ideas of individual and progressive men. He expresses that other dichotomy, the blindness of people who are otherwise highly intelligent, to aesthetic values and to real quality in design; and also the widely accepted importance of a literary-based educational system at the expense of developing tactile, visual and graphic understanding. Since Lethaby wrote his essay, however, new horological technology has swept away traditional types of clock movement, and has developed new materials and new standards for the design of clock cases too, though it has taken over half a century to do it.

Hood and dial of a longcase chiming clock; case in mahogany with elongated swan's-neck pediment and satyr's mask; dial plate covered with scrolled, engraved and pierced ornament; applied Arabic numerals; maker unknown; about 1900. *Stuart Hall Collection*

MODERN TIMES
Art Deco and the Electronic Age

The name 'Art Deco' is derived from the title of that great exhibition of art and design which was held in Paris in 1925, *L'Exposition Internationale des Arts Décoratifs et Industriels Modernes*, and has stuck as a descriptive term for that style of design accepted as 'modern' during the period between the wars, in the 1920s and 30s. As an all-embracing description of the many strands and aspects of the design of that period it is not really satisfactory, and now, 50 years later, the name Art Deco tends to be applied to what is otherwise known as *kitsch*, the ephemeral, precocious and superficial attempt to create a new 'style' as a reaction to the revivals of earlier styles which have been described in the eighth and ninth chapters. Yet within Art Deco itself there are to be found strands of, and re-interpretations from, the Edwardian era of Art Nouveau, particularly from the geometric essays in design of C. R. Mackintosh, though it must be remembered that he was still designing furniture and textiles for a few years after the First World War.

Vital changes took place in European society after the catastrophe of the First World War, and life was never quite the same again. Social values had changed, women obtained the vote, the class structure was broken down as all classes of society had shared in the horrors of the conflict. Even as the designers in the closing decades of the 19th century had felt a need to release themselves from the chains of 'Gothic' or 'Classic' or other revivals, and had done so in their own way, the need for change and a new outlook was all the more imperative in the new world after 1918. It was a time when the ordinary man and woman was felt to be worthy of a better quality of life, a better standard of domestic surroundings, a home for every family on the expanding housing estates, and a new life style which saw the coming of the popular motor car, the vacuum cleaner, the radio, the cinema, longer holidays, a broader and more extended education for all irrespective of income. The new society of the 1920s and '30s was based on an enormous expansion of the factory system, a system of cheap mass-production to which men and women were still chained in spite of their new-found 'freedom', so imaginatively satyrised by Charles Chaplin in the film *Modern Times*, made in 1938. It was a complex period of changing values and the styles of clock cases took on a new look, just as did everything else.

To attempt to simplify a most complex interaction of ideas which took place in design between the two European world wars is not easy, but the styles of design which emerged can, perhaps, be summed up as a fusion of four basic strands. The first of these was the 'modern' architectural style which relied on simple geometric forms arising from the use of new materials and building techniques, and owing allegiance to the doctrine of functionalism as preached by that famous school of design, founded by Walter Gropius at Weimar in Germany in 1919, known as the Bauhaus. The second was a desire for colour and texture in everyday objects, as well as good structure, which is at all times a basic human need. It owed something to the past but also owed a good deal to many

Mantel clock in oak with black stencilled decoration; mother of pearl dial; central mirror; designed by C. R. Mackintosh; 1919. *British Museum, London*

painters, sculptors and designers of the modern school such as Piet Mondrian (1872–1944), and to the ideas published in a journal called *De Stijl* (The Style) founded in 1917 by the Dutch artists Theo van Doesburg (1883–1931) and Gerrit Rietveld (1888–1964). Thirdly there was the desire for decoration, ornament and pattern which is perhaps best described today as 'Art Deco' in the *kitsch* sense, and which continued to look backwards for its inspiration, to Egyptian, Aztec and Oriental design. But finally, and perhaps most important of all, it was the use of newly available materials such as chromium plate, celluloid and bakelite which, added to new technology, changed the appearance of clocks as it did many other household objects. For example the development of either battery or mains powered electric clocks for domestic use, although not absolutely new to the period, constituted something of a revolution in domestic timekeeping. Some reference to these four different strands or influences will be made in describing but a few of the almost endless range of clock designs which came on the market in the 1920s and '30s. Almost all the examples chosen are now regarded as 'quality' pieces, the best of their kind but not typical of the cheap and often tawdry millions of clocks which were in everyday use.

Two clocks which may serve to indicate one of many directions taken by designers in the Art Deco style are illustrated, both being made of natural stone and both surmounted by sculptured female figures. The embellishment of clock cases with female figures was nothing new to French clock case design but the treatment of the figures on these clocks indicate changes of taste and attitudes which came about after the First World War.

The pyramidal, stepped form of the case of the first clock, dominated by a figure by the Rumanian-born sculptor Demetre Chiparus, working in France, is directly inspired by Mexican Aztec art, from the basic shape of an Aztec temple on top of which ritual human sacrifices took place. Some knowledge of the ancient Aztec culture of Mexico had been revealed to Europe in the days of the Spanish *conquistadores* in the 16th century, but it was not until political struggles had to some extent emancipated the Mexican peasants, under the New Constitution of 1917, that Europeans really began to take a new interest in Mexican affairs, and European influence began to be felt in Mexico too. Aldous Huxley (1894–1963) and D. H. Lawrence (1885–1930) both wrote on Mexican themes, the latter travelling widely in Mexico and being inspired to write his novel *The Plumed Serpent* of 1926. There was something mysterious and exciting about the life of the long-gone Aztec peoples, and their pictographic art which was devoid of naturalism in the European sense appealed to artists who were exploring new means of expression.

In the Chiparus clock, the polished marble base of triangular form with horizontal 'steps' is cut with hard, geometric precision and with a sturdy rigidity which to some extent echoes similar virtues in French black marble mantel clocks of the 19th century. Such decoration as is found on the surface of the stone and on the cast-metal, square dial, is composed of roughly hewn cuts derived from highly stylised palm fronds, and the numerals are chunky and bold, in high relief. In complete contrast to the weight and strength of the polished stone base, the bronze and ivory figure above is delicately detailed in hierarchic splendour, symmetrically posed in regal elegance, commanding the top of the case like some noble priestess of ancient times, and not unlike many of the mascots which embellished the radiators of cars in the 1920s and '30s. Even more like a car mascot is the figure by F. Preiss on a square, green onyx clock case of which the skeletonised dial, and especially the hands, remind one of much earlier styles. With her head thrown back and leaning on outstretched arms, she is similar to the classically inspired and well-known mascot figure on veteran Rolls-Royce cars, yet here she is in modern dress, with bobbed and not flowing hair, symbolic of the modern 'miss'. The short skirt, short hair, almost defiant nonchalant posture of this figure, in spirit repeated again and again on printed calendars or stands for table lamps, characterises the new-found freedom of women in the post First World War era, and also expresses the exotic, luxurious and expensive. Such luxury from the fashion-conscious world of London, Paris, New York and Hollywood was curiously at variance with the drab and monotonous, not to say poverty-stricken, world of many working-class people during the Great Depression, for whom 'make-believe' worlds were only available through the medium of the cinema. Amongst the housing estates and suburban sprawl of the 1930s the cinema had become the symbol of a new kind of freedom, and the new architecture of the cinema in its 'popular palace' style may be seen later in this chapter in an example from the 1930s, fitted with a modern turret clock.

In the 1925 catalogue of the French clock manufacturing firm of Favre–Bulle et Cie. item Y124 illustrates a mantel clock in the Art Deco style, of which an original example is shown. Its case is of inverted pyramidal form with symmetrical upward thrusting wedges at the sides creating a 'sunrise rays' effect which was an extremely popular decorative device at that time, in the rails of garden gates, for the leaded glass of semi-detached front doors, for the fret-cut designs of wireless loud-

Mantel clock in polished green onyx with a figure in bronze and ivory; figure by F. Preiss; about 1920

Mantel clock in polished marble with a figure in bronze and ivory; cast metal dial; figure by D. Chiparus; about 1925. *Victoria and Albert Museum, London*

145

speaker cabinets. The marquetry front of the clock case, incorporating metal scrolls and stylised flowers, is something of a throw back to the manner of Boulle and its ivory feet add a touch of quality. The 'Bulle' clock was an extremely popular early type of electrically powered clock, pioneered by M. Moulin and M. Favre-Bulle before the First World War, becoming commercially available from 1922 onwards. The illustrated catalogue of 1925 shows a wide range of case styles, from conventional circular dial clocks for the school or office, to the typically French 'four glass' case which owed its origin to the early 19th-century régulateur de cheminée; to Neo-Classical revival cases with inlaid shells, paterae, festoons, and ribbons of Adam derivation; to portico clock designs, again of early 19th-century French design and even to a complete reproduction case in the style of Louis XIV! Most typical of Bulle clock designs are the geometric, rectangular, square-dialled, marble, onyx and metal cases, with 'Aztec' derived ornament, with applied castings of flying birds, with sun-ray bursts and with electrical zig-zag devices.

The Bulle clock was but one of a number of domestic clocks powered by electrical energy, and it was copied under the trade name of 'Tempex' in England, marketed by British Horo-Electric Ltd, with glass dome and bakelite base. Another popular electrically powered clock was known as the Eureka, which appeared many years before the Bulle

Mantel clock with translucent glass front containing an electric movement by the firm of Léon Hattot (ATO); small electric lamps inside illuminated the case; glass panel produced by press moulding, this example being called 'Les Mésanges' (the tom-tits); about 1925–30

and was, in fact, a product of the Edwardian era. Invented in 1906 by T. B. Powers in the United States, its movement combined something of the traditional timekeeping properties of the oscillating balance with the impulsing of electrical energy, but it was housed in cases which owed their style to earlier architectural inspiration such as the one shown here, with Adam style inlays and Sheraton urn finials. The Eureka clock was only made for a few years, from 1906 to 1914, when about 10 000 units were produced in Clerkenwell, London.

Less well known than the Bulle or Eureka, the ATO electric clock was another product of the inter-war years. First produced in 1923, two basic movements were developed by the firm of Léon Hattot (ATO), both based on the same electrical principles as the Bulle but with

Mantel clock; case of rosewood and
nickel marquetry veneer with ivory feet;
movement by Favre-Bulle & Cie.,
Boulogne; 1925. *City Museum, Sheffield*

important differences as to the arrangement of the working parts. The
ATO movement was housed in a wide range of case styles, as was the
Bulle, 49 models appearing in the ATO catalogue. Some of the cases
were made of those materials which were typical of the 1920s and '30s,
bakelite and celluloid, and the company enlisted the skills of a famous
French glassmaker, René Jules Lalique (1860–1945). Lalique first
studied jewellery, but later he turned his attention to glass, and after the
First World War his factory at Wingen-sur-Moder produced distinctively etched and frosted, power-pressed glass plaques and panels, items
such as perfume flasks for Coty and even decorative car radiator caps.
For the ATO clock company his contribution was to design coloured
glass 'wings', decorated with animal forms in thick relief which were
illuminated from the rear by two 6-watt bulbs. The facility and ease
with which individual light sources could be provided in domestic
interiors by using electrical power, was one of the most characteristic
contributions to changes in interior design in the 1920s and '30s.

Electrically powered clocks of the 19th and 20th centuries were
mostly driven from small, low powered electric cells or batteries, but by
the early 1930s the mains electric synchronous clock had appeared on
the market due to the increasing availability of electrical power from the
central generating grid. The 'mains' clock depends for its timekeeping
on a motor, designed to run with a frequency dependent on the frequency of the public electricity supply, geared down to provide conventional time indication on a dial. Strictly speaking, it is not a clock at all,
the real 'clock' being the generating frequency of the supplying power
station. The main disadvantages of the mains clock were its need for a
constant physical connection to the power source of the building in
which it was used, and its vulnerability to any interruptions or cuts in
that supply. For some 40 years, however, it has remained a popular
clock, and is still frequently seen today, but the recent development of
electric cells, of small size and great reliability, linked with quartz-
crystal clock movement technology, is now undermining the use of the
mains clock, being free of the disadvantages inherent in their design.

Mantel clock known as the Eureka;
electrically operated movement; inlaid
mahogany case; made by the Eureka
Clock Company Limited, London; about
1912. *Hamlyn Group*

Mantel clock with conventional striking movement; oak veneered plywood case; chromium-plated bezel, hands and numerals; matt cream coloured dial with silvered decoration; made by the Bentima Clock and Watch Company, London; about 1950

Two early 'mains' clocks are shown, and in both examples the characteristic styles of the 1930s may be seen. The Everett Edgcumbe & Co. 'Synclock' of about 1931 is in a case of architectural simplicity, with flat stepped mouldings and of good proportion, eschewing those idiosyncracies of Art Deco seen in the Bulle and ATO examples, and perhaps owing something of its severe geometric simplicity to the work of the architects and furniture designers of the Bauhaus School, yet not quite freeing itself from the traditional use of natural timber and its associated mouldings. Far more characteristic of the Art Deco style is the clock marketed by Smiths English Clocks Ltd of Cricklewood, London, in its mirror-glass case with applied cut and etched decoration, its engine-turned copper-finish dial and its veneered wooden base. Manufactured in the 1930s, this clock makes use of one of the most popular of Art Deco materials, decorative mirror-glass, universally used in hotel foyers, in dining rooms and restaurants, in bathrooms and bars. The glitter and shine created an unreal world of luxury and splendour, and its introduction on an architectural scale was made possible by new and cheaper flat-glass making technology. In this small electric clock we see in miniscule the same decorative devices as were becoming widely used on engraved, etched and sand-blasted glass

Above left
Mantel clock with a mains electricity powered movement; oak case; trade name Synclock; made by Everett Edgcumbe and Company Limited, London; about 1930. *Crown Copyright. Science Museum, London*

Above right
Electric mantel clock finished in mirror glass with cut and etched decoration; engine-turned copper dial; made by Smiths English Clocks Limited, London; about 1930. *The Geffrye Museum, London*

doors and mirrors in public buildings. The front of the case is embellished with cut and polished stylised flowers and leaves, and the concave sides have etched upon them a pair of symmetrically disposed seminude figures, reminding one vividly of a similar use of such figures in French clocks of the Empire period. These figures on the Smiths clock, distinctive of the 1930s, stop well short of being banal, though they now appear extremely 'dated', and they belong to a period which could not quite free itself from a classical ancestry, for these figures have a flavour of ancient Crete or archaic Greece. The engine-turned copper dial of the Smiths clock takes us back to the portico clock of the Empire period and the skeletonised chapter ring is similar to that on the clock by Preiss.

On a more popular and humble scale it must not be forgotten that a vast range of ordinary clocks with traditional mechanical movements were being made in the 1920s and '30s, and continue to be made today. One of a type which was relatively cheaply produced, and which graced the sitting rooms of millions of ordinary homes, is a mantel clock distributed by the Bentima Clock and Watch Company of London, in the period both before and after the Second World War. This clock, made in the early 1950s, but stylistically belonging to the late 1930s, has a reliable eight-day movement by Perivale, with striking on a gong and a platform escapement, housed in a glued, plywood case of 'Napoleon hat' style, and finished with 'antique' faded oak veneer and a mass-produced decorative moulding on the front lower edge, redolent of Art Deco. Chromium plate is used for the bezel, and the dial centre with silvered floral scrolls on a matt cream ground, with embossed arabic numerals, has several features which link it to a traditional past. The chromium-plated hands are pure Art Deco in style.

Although millions of cheap and popular domestic clocks continued to be made with conventional mechanical movements after the Second World War, various forms of electrically powered and electronic movements have gradually begun to take over, and the days of mechanical clocks with conventional mainsprings and escapements are undoubtedly numbered in the modern world of the micro-chip and miniature transistor. A few models of highly distinctive quality and superb mechanical craftsmanship, however, have continued to be produced since the 1920s, of which the Atmos clock is a good example. Made in Switzerland, the clock depends for its self-winding action on small changes of temperature and barometric pressure, and the quality of its simple and dignified casework and its precision movement, firmly establishes such a timepiece in the finest horological tradition, with its aesthetic appeal of a visible movement linking it to the early 19th-century French régulateur. The use of small electric currents produced by the action of light falling on to a light-sensitive cell also produced a number of finely made and very expensive clocks by such firms as Patek Philippe of Switzerland and Kienzle of Germany. One example by the latter firm is in the finest tradition of modern architectural design, its elegance depending entirely on its proportions and quality of finish.

Although both the Atmos clock and the light clock rely on advanced technology, there also continues a demand for the finest quality of traditional clockwork, and there could be no better example than one of the range of clocks with chronometer movements produced by Thomas Mercer Chronometers Limited, formerly of St Albans but now based in Cheltenham. With a history dating back to the early decades of the 19th century, the Thomas Mercer company has manufactured thousands of marine chronometers. Today its latest clock, for domestic use, is the elegant dignified model known as the 'Cheltenham' which combines the magnificent quality of a chronometer movement

Mantel clock with gilded bronze and glass case, known as the Atmos clock; made by Jaeger-le-Coultre, Switzerland; about 1935. *City Museum, Sheffield*

Above
Mantel or carriage clock with chronometer movement, known as The Cheltenham; made by Thomas Mercer (Chronometers) Limited, Cheltenham; 1982. *Courtesy of Thomas Mercer Ltd*

Left
Mantel clock powered by natural light; trade name Heliomat; made by Kienzle, Germany; about 1970. *Hamlyn Group*

Table or desk clock in a black plastic case; the movement is an advanced form of constant force escapement, battery powered and made in Switzerland under the trade name Selticon; case designed in Italy; about 1965. *Merseyside County Museums, Liverpool*

Small portable digital alarm and chronograph clock which announces the time at the touch of a button; satin-finished case; made by the Sharp Corporation; Japan; 1981

with a clean and well proportioned polished brass case, based on the traditional design of the carriage clock. Undoubtedly, there is still a demand for clocks of this type which satisfy the desire for a finely designed and manufactured mechanism and superlative case, over and above the ordinary practical requirement of being able to tell the time.

A post Second World War domestic clock, which promised much in the way of linking clock case design with modern ideas in the world of the arts, was the plastic moulded table or desk clock designed by Mangiarotti and Marassutti in Italy in the 1960s. Its smooth, rounded pedestal form was clearly inspired by the aesthetic awareness of the satisfying nature of rounded, water-worn pebbles and rocks when held in the hand, to which attention had been drawn by, amongst others, two great English sculptors Barbara Hepworth (1903–75) and Henry Moore (*b* 1898) through the nature and quality of the sculptures they produced. The clock contained an electrically powered sophisticated constant-force escapement movement known as the Selticon, and two basic types of case were produced, one being the pedestal form seen here and the other a rounded, pebble-like form which sat comfortably low on the table. One of the most satisfying designs of 20th-century clock dials was produced for these Selticon movements, in which the hours were marked by a pair of parallel batons which gradually increase in thickness from 1 to 12. This subtlety of design, linked with harmonious proportions, suggests a clockwise movement of the kind which had been attempted experimentally by C. R. Mackintosh over 40 years earlier. Not unrelated in style to the Mangiarotti Marassutti clock is the little rounded plastic cased alarm clock with a conventional spring powered movement at only a fraction of the price of the Italian model, pleasant to hold, jolly and even amusing, and a product of the new 'Pop' culture of the 1970s (see p. 136).

Digital dial of a station clock in the public concourse area; 1980

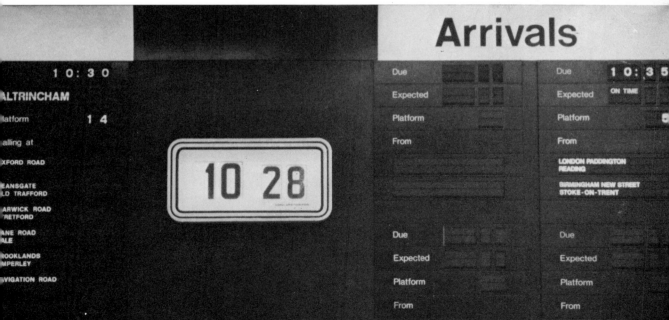

In former times repeat striking clocks dating from the late 17th century, along with various designs of illuminated dials, endeavoured to provide the time at night, and today the world is full of clocks which provide a permanently-lit digital display of the time through light-emitting diodes (LED). The world of electronics has also recently provided the speaking clock whose synthesised voice announces the time at the touch of a button, and also includes musical alarms, time interval measuring facilities and spoken hour and half hour indicators. Clocks such as these with constant digital time indication through a liquid crystal display (LCD), and clocks associated with radios, television sets, video-recorders, domestic ovens and countless other articles brings us into the world of the 1980s, in which new technology is inaugurating a new industrial revolution. This is proving to be as fundamental and important to western society as was the last industrial revolution of the 18th and 19th centuries.

The digital dial for clocks has to some extent been slow to make its appeal to the general public, for the conventional analogue dial is a far more direct and graphic representation of the division of the day or night. The digital dial requires a thought process between recognising the figures and interpreting what they mean, whereas the analogue dial is recognisable at a glance. Gradually and imperceptibly, however, people are becoming accustomed to the new presentation, and the digital dial in its 24-hour cycle, is taking over the field.

The Westminster Clock, popularly known as Big Ben; dial and hands designed by the architect Sir Charles Barry for the Palace of Westminster, London; 1859. *Crown Copyright—reproduced with permission of the Controller of HMSO*

Dial of a clock in a cast-iron frame with translucent glass panels typical of many thousands of 19th-century turret clock dials. *By Smiths of Derby*

To return to the tower, or turret clock, last mentioned in the first chapter, this type of clock is still widely seen on public buildings but they are far more frequently noted not to be working than once was the case. The public clock is of much less importance now than in Victorian and former times, for people today have almost universal access to the wristlet watch, and to a time standard provided by the GPO telephone system, and by radio and television time announcements. Some clocks, like the famous Westminster clock (popularly but wrongly known as Big Ben, which is the name of the hour bell, so-called after Sir Benjamin Hall, Chief Commissioner at the time of its erection) have become national symbols, recognisable by all and held in affectionate respect. To be fully serviceable by both day and night Victorian tower clocks, like the Westminster clock, had illuminated dials made of translucent opal glass fitted into an iron skeleton frame, and the design of such dials belongs to architectural rather than domestic realms.

Tower clocks have rarely been mentioned in this book since their movements have no decorative appeal because of their hidden locations. Some mediaeval and later turret clock frames were embellished with finials and mouldings of a decorative nature, and occasionally 'architectural' detailing is found at a later date. Although the earliest of 'public'

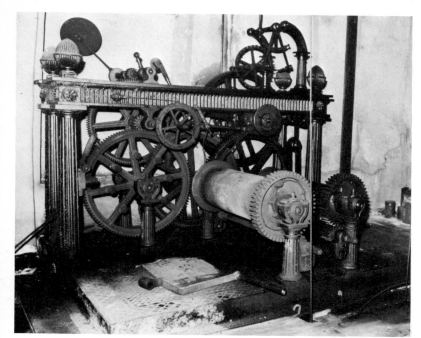

clocks had no dials at all, but conveyed their message through the striking of bells, by the 16th century dials began to appear, and the 17th and 18th centuries saw the evolution of various types. As with early domestic clocks, turret clock dials were at first single-handed, square in form and made of wood, stone and sometimes iron. By the 18th century the square dial was frequently mounted as a diamond, while octagonal dials also had their place. The 19th-century cast-iron, skeletonised dial had arrived, largely through the availability of public lighting, once gas (and later electricity) supplies were assured. In the 20th century it has been common to omit a 'dial' as a separate architectural entity, but rather to indicate the time by means of plain, evenly spaced batons for the chapters, and plain hands mounted directly on the surface of a wall. Illumination of such dials is easily achieved by means of fluorescent strip lights. Another artificially lit type of public time indication is by the display of digital numerals on a panel made up of an appropriate arrangement of electric light bulbs. This method has been used in American cities for many years, frequently displaying the time for a short interval and alternating this display with one showing the prevailing temperature.

A survival of a public clock from about 1930 still stands on the Aberystwyth sea front in central Wales, though alas many such clocks are fast disappearing. The Aberystwyth clock is in the tower of what was once a cinema, but is now a Bingo Hall. The 'stepped' architectural mass of the tower, geometric and severe, crowned by a flagstaff and with long vertical windows and triangular fluted mouldings to enhance the design, is pure Art Deco. It reminds one forcibly of a famous London landmark of much larger scale, the tower of the Wembley Stadium which was opened in 1924, the venue of the British Empire Exhibition and still the home of important sporting events. The clock at Aberystwyth, with illuminated batons instead of numerals, driven by a synchronous electric mechanism, is a relic from an era which is now passing into history, which has gone through those years when its style was rejected as sham and vulgar, and which is now coming into its own with a nostalgia for days which will never return again.

Throughout this book emphasis has been placed on the relationships which exist between the design of clock cases and the world of the artist, the designer and the architect. As the nature of life today is being shaped by electronic devices, by computers and space technology, and as old values are breaking down, perhaps our concepts of 'art' are breaking down too. It is astonishing to read the words of Theo van Doesburg, written in 1926 in a manifesto called *The End of Art* for the journal *De Stijl*. With his extraordinary foresight and perception it is as if van Doesburg knew, nearly 60 years ago, that clocks and other domestic furnishings as 'works of decorative art' were becoming things of the past, as though he knew about the functional electronic devices which were to come:

'One cannot renew Art. "Art" is an invention of the Renaissance which has today refined itself to the utmost degree possible. An enormous concentration was needed to make good works of Art. One could only develop this concentration by neglecting life (as in religion) or to lose life entirely. That is today impossible for we are only interested in life.

Let's refresh ourselves with things that are not Art: the bathroom, the W.C., the bathtub, the telescope, the bicycle, the auto, the subways, the flat-iron, [the clock?[1]]. There are many people who know how to make such good unartistic things. But they are hindered, and their movements are dictated by the priests of Art. Art, whose function nobody knows, hinders the function of life. For the sake of progress we must destroy Art. Because the function of modern life is stronger than Art, every attempt to renew Art (Futurism, Cubism, Expressionism) failed. They are all bankrupt. Let us not waste our time with them. Let us rather create a new life-form which is adequate to the functioning of modern life.'

[1] Inserted by the author.

Glossary of Terms

Architectural and furniture terms relating to clock case design, including a few technical horological details

ACANTHUS
: A stylised leaf motif used on Corinthian capitals and extensively employed in other decorative ways; of Greek origin.

ACROTERIA
: A pair of ornamental carved features, of foliate design, on the ends of a classical pediment.

AMORINI
: Alternative name for cherubs or cupids, frequently found in classical and Renaissance art.

ANTHEMION
: A type of ornament of related form to the honeysuckle flower, much used in Neo-Classical design; of Greek origin.

APRON
: The lower front member of a cabinet or clock case, between the feet, usually ornamented and curved.

ARABESQUE
: Linear ornament applied to a flat surface, composed of scrolls, leaves, tendrils, flowers, animals, vases etc; done in various media.

ARCADE
: *Arcading* A range of arches supported on columns in a continuous manner, either free-standing or 'blind' when attached to a wall.
: *Arcaded minutes* A minute circle on some clock dials in which the divisions for each five-minute space are arcaded.

ARCH
: *O-gee* Composed of convex and concave curves, drawn from four centres to produce a sharply pointed apex.
: *Pointed* Composed of two segments of a circle, drawn from two centres to meet at a point at the top.
: *Segmental* Another name for a pointed arch.
: *Semi-circular* Constructed in a single half-circle, sometimes with a large stone, known as the key-stone, at the top.

ARCHITRAVE
: The lowest member of an entablature (q.v.) usually plain.

BALANCE
: The last member of the wheel train of a portable clock which, by its oscillations, controls the timekeeping. In early clocks known as a wheel balance.

BALUSTER
: A small column or pillar, variously formed according to period, style and material.

BALUSTRADE
: A series of balusters supporting a handrail or coping on a building or staircase.

BELL-TOP
: *True* The top of a bracket clock with a convex moulding (ovolo—q.v.) above a concave moulding (cavetto—q.v.)
: *Inverted* The top of a bracket clock with a concave moulding above a convex moulding—an earlier form than the true bell-top.

BEZEL
: A ring or frame, usually of metal, supporting the glass for a clock dial, hinged at one side.

BLUING
: A type of heat treatment to produce a blue finish on polished steel.

BRACKET
: Either a supporting projection from a wall to carry a clock, or a projecting member of a cabinet supporting a horizontal member.

BRACKET FOOT A moulded foot for a longcase or bracket clock in wood or metal, shaped like a bracket and projecting on the outside edge.

BREAK ARCH The name given to a dial aperture in which the upper part is semi-circular.

BUN FOOT A type of ball foot, of flattened form, introduced in the second half of the 17th century.

BUTTRESS A projection of masonry on the outside of a building to give additional strength at the main stress points.
Flying buttress Used mainly in Gothic buildings the flying buttress carries the stress of the nave vault to the main buttress, through segmental arches.
Buttress offset The steps or stages by which the buttress is increased in thickness towards the base.

CANOPY A projection or hood, commonly over altars, pulpits, niches, choir-stalls etc., and over some clocks.

CAPITAL The upper member or top of a column, of various forms.

CARCASE The name given to the essential basic structure of a clock case or piece of furniture, without veneer (q.v.) or other finish.

CARTOUCHE An enclosure or panel with an ornamental frame, often containing an inscription.

CARYATID A female figure sculptured to form a column; much used in various styles, but derived from Greek architecture.

CASTING The process of producing ornamental or functional metallic shapes by pouring molten metal into a mould.

CATKIN Hanging plant form of willow or hazel, as a decorative feature in Neo-Classical design.

CHAMFER-TOP In clock cases the name applied to a gently sloping top, usually surmounted with a central finial.

CHAPTER RING The circular ring on a clock dial on which the hours and minutes are engraved or otherwise applied.

CHASING A term used to describe the ornamentation of metalwork by punching with blunt steel chasing tools.

CHISELLING A term used to describe the ornamentation of metal or wood by cutting with a sharp steel chisel.

COCK A bracket screwed to a clock movement which supports the pivot of one of its moving parts.
Beading This is a moulding of semi-circular section (astragal) used on the edges of longcase clock doors to hide the gap, or on drawer edges in chests of drawers.

COLONNADE A range or series of columns in line.

COLUMN A vertical architectural feature, consisting of capital, shaft and base; a pillar.
Corner column The name applied to a quarter column (q.v.) mostly used on longcase clock trunks.
Coupled column Composed of several shafts grouped together; a characteristic of Gothic architecture.
Detached column Used ornamentally in furniture, but free-standing.
Quarter column Of a quarter circle in section, used decoratively on longcase clock trunks (see corner columns).
Three quarter column A column used extensively on longcase clock hood doors, of three-quarters of a circle in section.

CONSOLE A projecting bracket usually of scrolled form, supporting the upper members of an entablature (q.v.).

CORBEL Primarily an architectural term meaning a bracket.

CORNICE The upper, moulded, projecting member of the entablature (q.v.), or top projecting moulding in cabinetwork.

CRESTING The carved decoration above the cornice found on late 17th century longcase clock hoods, on chair backs etc.

CROCKET A decorative leaf-shaped feature found on the sloping edges of pinnacles, spires and gables in Gothic architecture.

CUPOLA A small turret on the top of a roof, usually circular or polygonal.

CUSPING The pointed projections dividing the foils on the inner side of a Gothic arch.

DADO The decorative division of the lower part of a wall (interior).

DECAL This is an American term for the transfer designs used on the glass tablets of popular American clocks.

DIAL PLATE The base or back plate of a clock dial, to which the chapter ring (q.v.) and spandrels (q.v.) are fitted.

DOME A hemi-spherical feature used on buildings in prominent positions, over a square bay; also used for the top or hood of a clock, or glass shade for a skeleton clock.

EBONISE To stain an inferior wood black in order to make it resemble ebony.

ENAMELLING A heat process of fusing or vitrifying glass-like compounds on to copper; much used in clock dials. Also applies to colours fired on to enamel ground or porcelain.

ENGRAVING A term used to describe the ornamentation of a metal surface by cutting a groove into it with an engraver's burin.

ENTABLATURE The upper portion of any of the architectural orders (q.v.) consisting of the cornice, frieze and architrave.

ENTASIS This is the slight outward curving of the sides of a column; originally used by the Greeks to prevent the optical illusion of concavity in the column.

FAÇADE The principal frontage of a building.

FASCES A type of border ornament derived from a bundle of rods strapped together; a Neo-Classical feature of Roman origin.

FESTOON A suspended wreath of flowers, leaves etc; much used in Neo-Classical design and sometimes known as a swag (q.v.).

FILIGREE Fine ornamental work in wire, usually of gold or silver, in intricate patterns or tracery.

FINIAL An ornamental feature on the top of a building or piece of furniture; the topmost member of a pinnacle (q.v.).

FLUTING Vertical grooving or channelling on a column or pilaster (q.v.).

FOLIAGE Whence foliated—any grouping or arrangement of leaves, stems as a decorated embellishment.

FRET An open, pierced frieze, gallery or other member, often but not always of geometric design.
Blind fret A pierced strip or frieze glued down to a solid member.

FRIEZE Architecturally this is the middle member of an entablature (q.v.) but is used more generally to denote an upper division of decoration on furniture or interiors.

GARLAND A loosely draped wreath of leaves and flowers as distinct from a formally arranged festoon (q.v.).

GESSO A preparation composed of whiting, linseed oil and glue as a base to lacquer work and gilding.

GILDING	The decoration of ornament by the application of pure gold, either as water-gilding on wood, or mercurial gilding on metal.
GRIFFIN	A fabulous and mythical beast with head and wings of an eagle; used heraldically and derived from mediaeval bestiaries.
GRILLE	A metal lattice-work plate, in clocks often used backed with fabric to permit the sound of the bell to be heard.
GROTESQUE	A fanciful ornamental decoration, devised to be deliberately fantastic, especially as applied to masks.
GUILLOCHE	An ornamental moulded design based on interlaced circles; in Neo-Classical design, and also more coarsely on earlier oak furniture.
HERM	A plain column or pilaster with the head of a man at the top; derived from Greek sources depicting the god Hermes.
HONEYSUCKLE	A formalised frieze pattern based on the honeysuckle flower; of Greek origin—(see Anthemion).
HOOD	The upper, removable part of a longcase clock cabinet, or sometimes the canopy over certain types of Dutch clocks.
HUSKING	A popular type of Neo-Classical ornament based on the outer covering of fruit or seeds, arranged either in festoons or vertical hangings of diminishing size.
INLAY	Ornamentation sunk into a flat surface, of either wood, metal or other materials.
INTARSIA	Derived from the Italian *tarsia*, this is a form of pictorial design based on the use of different kinds of inlaid woods.
JAPANNING	The name given to English imitation of Oriental lacquer.
LABEL	In horological terms the name applied by American clock designers to the manufacturer's trade-paper, pasted inside the case.
.LACQUER	A type of polished, lustrous finish based on the use of certain resins, originating in the Far East and copied, in inferior ways, in the West.
LANCET	A tall Gothic window with pointed arch; also applied to certain clocks with pointed arched tops.
LINTEL	The top, horizontal member of a door or window opening.
MARQUETRY	A decorative use of veneering (q.v.) in which elaborate patterns are produced.
	Arabesque marquetry A type in which complex patterns of leaves, flowers, birds, vases etc. are used (see arabesque).
	Endive marquetry A type of extremely fine pattern based on or resembling the endive leaf.
	Oystershell marquetry A type in which oppositely matching pairs of thin veneers from the boughs of laburnum or walnut are placed to resemble open oystershells.
	Seaweed marquetry Another name for extremely fine patterns of marquetry, similar to endive (q.v.).
MASK	A face, of human or animal form, used as a decorative device.
MEDALLION	A circular, oval or rectangular plaque in low relief; applied particularly to Wedgwood jasperware inlays in furniture and clocks.
MOULDING	A continuous projection or projecting member in architecture or furniture design, of various sections, to enhance and punctuate the whole design.
	Bead moulding A continuous repetition of bead forms (like a string of beads) to make a moulding.
	Cavetto moulding A moulding of hollow or concave section, based on the quadrant of a circle.

Cyma-recta moulding A type of o-gee moulding, convex in the lower part and concave in the upper.

Cyma-reversa moulding The reverse arrangement of cyma-recta.

Dentil moulding A moulding made up of a series of small rectangular blocks, like teeth: derived from Greek architecture.

Egg and dart moulding A continuous repetition moulding of alternate forms of beads and arrow heads. Known also as egg and anchor or egg and tongue.

Ovolo moulding The name for a wide convex moulding of quarter-round section.

MOUNT In furniture and clocks (especially French) the name applied to metal ornamental castings added to the basic form, and usually gilded.

MULLION A vertical supporting member of the frame of a window.

OBELISK A tapering, square shaft with pyramidal top; used architecturally in monumental form and also as the basis of some clock cases, case ornaments and other decorative items.

ORDER OF ARCHITECTURE The classification of various types of Greek and Roman architectural arrangements of entablature, capital, column, base, plinth; as follows:

Doric An early Greek design of simple fluted shaft with no base; the Roman variant was of more slender proportion with a base to the column, and plain shaft.

Ionic Used by both Greeks and Romans, this order is most easily distinguished by the spirally curved volutes on the capital of the column.

Corinthian Also used by both Greeks and Romans, having a complex capital made up of elaborately arranged acanthus (q.v.) leaves.

Tuscan A Roman derivative of the Greek Doric order, but having a base to the column. The Tuscan order was much employed by Renaissance clock case designers.

Composite A Roman variant in which the volutes of the Ionic are combined with the acanthus leaves of the Corinthian in the design of the capitals.

ORMOLU Literally, from the French, 'ground gold', this is used to describe the gilded bronze or brass of French furniture and clock mounts (q.v.).

PAGODA TOP Derived from the form of an Oriental pagoda, this is applied to the concave curved shape of some clock tops in the 'chinoiserie' manner.

PARAPET A low wall at the edge of a roof; occasionally for similar features in furniture design.

PARQUETRY This is a simple, geometric form of marquetry (q.v.), using star shapes, triangles etc. either as a veneer or sometimes as inlay.

PATERAE Small ornamental discs of round or oval form, in Neo-Classical design.

PATINA The natural finish on the surface of wood or metal acquired after many years of exposure, use and handling; regarded as important and not to be destroyed by over-zealous cleaning.

PEDESTAL Architecturally a support or plinth, used by furniture designers for any solid support for lamps, clocks etc.

PEDIMENT The low-pitched gable end of a classical temple, in Renaissance architecture, furniture design and clock cases, in several forms.

Broken pediment One in which the centre is left open to accommodate a centred urn, spire or sculptural figure.

Hollow pediment One in which the upper portion has deep concave curves on each side; of Oriental inspiration.

Segmental pediment One in which the sloping sides are not straight, but are segments of a circle, or in which the whole upper part is one complete segment.

Swan's neck pediment One in which the upper sides are shaped as double curved scrolls, terminating in the centre in two bosses.

Triangular pediment The basic classical shape which is a low-pitched isosceles triangle.

PENDANT A hanging ornamental feature, of various types of design.

PILASTER A 'flattened' column, rectangular in section, applied to a vertical surface but embracing the elements of the architectural 'order' to which it belongs.

PINEAPPLE A finial in the form of a pineapple; much used in Regency period clock designs and architecturally as a terminal to gate posts etc.

PINNACLE Not to be confused with a finial (q.v.) a pinnacle is usually associated with mediaeval architecture as a steep pyramidal or conical form above buttresses or at the corners of a tower.

PLAQUE Another name for a porcelain or enamel panel in a clock case.

PLINTH The main architectural base of a piece of furniture, eg the wide lower portion of a longcase clock. In buildings the platform or foundation level on which the structure stands.

PORCELAIN A ceramic material fired to a high temperature; hard, white and translucent.

Biscuit This is the porcelain body first fired but not glazed. Clock cases of biscuit porcelain are usually protected by a glass dome or shade.

Glazed To protect porcelain from dirt and stains it is usually glazed with glassy materials which melt in a second firing.

Parian This is a particular variety of porcelain, so-called because of its resemblance to marble from the Greek island of Paros. Much used in the 19th century.

PORTICO The centre-piece of a house or church with columns, pediment etc. The name of a type of clock case so shaped.

QUATREFOIL An aperture or decorative feature composed of four rounded leaf shapes, or 'foils', separated by cusps (q.v.).

QUOINS Architecturally heavy projecting blocks of masonry at the corners of buildings; frequently simulated on the plinths of 18th century longcase clocks, and other furniture.

REEDING The reverse of fluting (q.v.), being a series of ribs standing in relief, side by side.

RELIEF Describes any feature or decoration standing proud of, or projecting from, a flat surface.

REPOUSSÉ A metal working technique for bringing a design or pattern into relief.

RESERVE A word rather loosely describing an area separated from its background; especially important in French clock dials where the numerals are often depicted in reserve panels.

ROSE WINDOW The name of a circular window, especially in French churches, with radiating ribs.

ROUNDEL Of wide application a roundel is used for many decorative features occupying a circular panel.

SHAFT The main part of a column, between the capital and base (see column).

SKELETONISE To cut away portions of clock movement plates not technically necessary; thus 'skeleton clock' with open-worked plates.

SPANDREL The decorative applied mounts at the four corners of a brass dial; also for painted or engraved dial corners between the chapter ring and edge.

SPHINX A mythical creature with the body of a lion, the head and bust of a woman and wings of a bird. An Egyptian sphinx was wingless. Much used in Empire and Regency decorative art.

SPIRE	Architecturally used for the pointed termination of a church tower, but in clock design for globular finials and other ornaments to decorate the top of the hood, sometimes incorporating an eagle.
STRAPWORK	A particular form of 16th and 17th century ornament making use of geometrically arranged bands and scrolls.
STRINGING	The technique of inlaying fine strips of wood of lighter tone than the ground wood to form linear inlay designs in clock cases and other furniture.
SWAG	Alternative name for a festoon (q.v.); of earlier use and frequently referring to a festoon of carved cloth.
TABLET	In American clocks the name given to the painted or transfer-decorated glass panels in the front of the cases.
TAZZA	A shallow Greek drinking vessel used decoratively on many clock cases of late 18th and early 19th-century design.
TORCH FINIAL	A finial (q.v.) in the form of a lighted torch, with stylised flames.
TRACERY	Pierced stone or woodwork creating ornamental patterns, especially relative to Gothic windows and Gothic Revival treatment.
TRAIN	The technical name for the arrangement of wheels and pinions to activate the going and striking of a clock.
TRANSOM	The horizontal members of a window frame; usually associated with mediaeval architecture (see mullion).
TREFOIL	An aperture or decorative feature composed of three rounded leaf shapes, or 'foils', separated by cusps (q.v.).
TRUNK	The main part, or body of a longcase clock, between hood and plinth.
TURNING	A method of reducing wood, stone, metal etc. to cylindrical or round section ornamental form; done on various types of lathe. *Twist turning* A particular form of ornamental turning in furniture of the late 17th century, known as 'spiral turning'.
TYMPANUM	The space or area inside a pediment, between the lintel and the upper edge.
VAULT	A method of roofing a building in stone, of many forms. The structure of ribs and panels occasionally appears in mediaeval furnishings and clock case designs.
VENEER	A thin sheet of fine quality wood (or sometimes other material) applied to the carcase (q.v.) of a clock case or other furniture to enhance the finish.
VITRUVIAN SCROLL	A type of Roman classical ornament or enrichment, of scrolled form embellished with acanthus leaves, named after the Roman architect Vitruvius.
WHIPLASH	The name applied to a type of writhing, convoluted line which is characteristic of much design in the Art Nouveau manner.

Select Bibliography

This bibliography mainly includes books which have been published in recent years, and concentrates on those in which considerable attention is given to clock case styles.

Allix, Charles, *Carriage Clocks*, London 1974

Bailey, Chris. H., *Two Hundred Years of American Clocks and Watches*, Englewood Cliffs, New Jersey 1975

Barker, David, *The Arthur Negus Guide to English Clocks*, London 1980

Bassermann-Jordan, Ernst von (revised by Hans von Bertele), *The Book of Old Clocks and Watches*, London 1964

Battison, Edwin A. and Kane, Patricia E., *The American Clock 1725–1865*, Greenwich, Connecticut 1973

Bellaigue, Geoffrey de, *The James A. Rothschild Collection at Waddesdon Manor—Furniture, Clocks and Gilt Bronzes* Vol. 1. National Trust 1974

Belmont, Henry L., *La Bulle-Clock: Horlogerie Électrique*, Besançon 1975

Bird, Anthony, *English House Clocks 1600–1850*, Newton Abbot 1973

Britten, F. J., (see Clutton, Baillie and Ilbert)

Bruton, Eric, *The History of Clocks and Watches*, London 1979

Bruton, Eric, *The Longcase Clock*, London 1977

Bruton, Eric, *The Wetherfield Collection of Clocks; A Guide to Dating English Antique Clocks*, London 1981

Cescinsky, H. and Webster, M. R., *English Domestic Clocks*, London 1913 (reprinted in facsimile 1976)

Clutton, C., Baillie, G. H. and Ilbert, C. A., *Britten's Old Clocks and Watches and their Makers*, London 8th Edition 1973

Collard, F. Bernard Royer-, *Skeleton Clocks*, London 1969

Coole, P. G. and Neumann, E., *The Orpheus Clocks*, London 1972

Dawson, Percy G., Drover, C. B. and Parkes, D. W., *Early English Clocks*, Woodbridge, Suffolk 1982

Distin, William H. and Bishop, Robert, *The American Clock: A Comprehensive Pictorial Survey, 1723–1900*, New York 1976

Edwardes, Ernest L., *The Grandfather Clock*, Altrincham 1971

Edwardes, Ernest L., *The Story of the Pendulum Clock*, Altrincham 1977

Edwardes, Ernest L., *Weight-driven Chamber Clocks of the Middle Ages and Renaissance*, Altrincham 1965

Edey, Winthrop, *French Clocks*, London 1967

Fleet, Simon, *Clocks*, London 1961

Goodison, Nicholas P., *Ormolu: The Work of Matthew Boulton*, London 1974

Guye, Samuel and Michel, Henri, *Time and Space: Measuring Instruments from the 15th to the 19th Century*, London 1971

Hawkins, J. B., *Thomas Cole and Victorian Clockmaking*, Sydney 1975

Jagger, Cedric, *The World's Great Clocks and Watches*, London 1977

Jagger, Cedric, *Royal Clocks. The British Monarchy and its Timekeepers 1300–1900*, London 1983

Lloyd, H. Alan, *The Collector's Dictionary of Clocks*, London 1964

Lloyd, H. Alan, *Old Clocks* (4th edition), London 1970

Lloyd, H. Alan, *Some Outstanding Clocks over 700 years: 1250–1950,* London 1958

Loomes, Brian, *Complete British Clocks*, Newton Abbot 1978

Loomes, Brian, *White Dial Clocks, The Complete Guide*, Newton Abbot 1981

Leopold, John H., *The Almanus Manuscript*, London 1971

Michel, Henri, *Scientific Instruments in Art and History* (translated by Francis R. and R. E. W. Maddison), London and New York 1967

Mody, N. H. N., *Japanese Clocks*, London 1932 (later edition n.d.)

Nemrava, Steve Z., *The Morbier 1680–1900*, Portland, Oregon 1975

Palmer, Brooks, *The Book of American Clocks*, New York 1950

Palmer, Brooks, *A Treasury of American Clocks*, New York 1967

Robinson, Tom, *The Longcase Clock*, Woodbridge, Suffolk 1981

Rose, Ronald E., *English Dial Clocks*, Woodbridge, Suffolk 1978

Sellink, J. L., *Dutch Antique Domestic Clocks*, Leiden 1973

Shenton, A. and Shenton, R., *The Price Guide to Clocks, 1840–1940,* Woodbridge, Suffolk 1977

Smith, Alan, *Clocks and Watches*, London 1975

Smith, Alan (Ed.), *The Country Life International Dictionary of Clocks,* London 1979

Symonds, R. W., *A Book of English Clocks*, London 1947

Symonds, R. W., *Masterpieces of English Furniture and Clocks*, London 1955

Symonds, R. W., *Thomas Tompion, his Life and Work*, London 1951

Tardy, H. Lengelle, *La Pendule Française*, Paris 1948–50, 3 volumes, various reprintings

Tyler, E. John, *Black Forest Clocks*, London 1977

Tyler, E. John, *American Clocks for the Collector*, London 1981

Ullyet, Kenneth, *In Quest of Clocks*, London 1950

Ullyet, Kenneth, *British Clocks and Clockmakers*, London 1947

Wilson, Gillian, *French 18th century Clocks in the J. Paul Getty Museum,* Malibu, California 1976

INDEX

References in bold type refer to illustrations.

Index compiled by the author.